Miscellanea Historiae Pontificiae

edita a Facultate Historiae Ecclesiasticae
in Pontificia Universitate Gregoriana
Vol. 55

Francesco Turvasi, M.S.C.

GIOVANNI GENOCCHI
AND
THE INDIANS OF SOUTH AMERICA
(1911-1913)

EDITRICE PONTIFICIA UNIVERSITÀ GREGORIANA

ROMA 1988

IMPRIMI POTEST

Romae die 28 Ianuarii 1988

R. P. GILLES PELLAND, S.J.
Rector Universitatis

IMPRIMATUR

✠ GIOVANNI MARRA, *Ausiliare*

Dal Vicariato di Roma, 30 maggio 1988

ISBN 88-7652-585-8

EDITRICE PONTIFICIA UNIVERSITÀ GREGORIANA
EDITRICE PONTIFICIO ISTITUTO BIBLICO
Piazza della Pilotta 35 - 00187 Roma, Italia

With gratitude
to the Reverend Father Francis Mulvanity

ACKNOWLEDGMENT

Many friends and colleagues read my manuscript and provided helpful comments and advice. I wish in particular to thank Msgr. Terzo Natalini, the Vice-Prefect of the Archivio Segreto Vaticano. Without his generous assistance and encouragement this book could never have been written.

CONTENTS

ABBREVIATIONS

AGG   Archives Giovanni Genocchi.
c/o the Author.

ACPF   Archives of the Congregation for the Propagation of the Faith:
"Peru, Ucayali".
Rome, Italy.

ASV.DP   Archivio Segreto Vaticano, Delegazione Apostolica in Peru:
"Msgr. Scapardini Angelo (1910-1917)", N. 75.
Vatican City State.

ASV.SS.   Archivio Segreto Vaticano, Segreteria di Stato: "Missione nel
Putumayo", 1913, Rub. 17.
Vatican City State.

PRO.FO   Public Record Office, Foreign Office: "Peru, Ecuador" (1909-1913).
London, England.

N.B. AGG is followed by the volume of the letters (L) or of the writings (S),
and the alphabetical section.

ACPF is followed by the number of the Rubrica (R) and the number of
the protocol of the document.

ASV.DP is followed by the number of the Fascicolo (F) and the number
of the page.

ASV.SS is followed by the number of the Fascicolo (F) and the number
of the page.

PRO.FO is followed simply by the number of the protocol.

The documents used in this work are of different languages. The most
important documents are in Latin or Italian (as those of the Roman Curia and
Father Genocchi's diplomatic reports). The documents collected by Fr. Genocchi
are in Spanish, French, German, and especially, in English.

With few exceptions the author thought it was not strictly necessary to
quote the original text or to put it in a footnote, because all the correspondence
and diaries of Fr. Genocchi, in their original form, are in the process of being
published.

PREFACE

"One of the most noble and beneficent accomplishments of the Pontificate of Pius X was the Holy See's energetic assistance to the Indian rubber gatherers who were the victims of cruel and brutal treatment at the hands of their white owners."[1] In these terms the eminent scholar, Giorgio Levi della Vida, former professor of Semitic and Islamic philology at the University of Pennsylvania, appraises the Pontificate of Pope Pius X, better known to historians for his condemnation of the modernist movement.

This undertaking of Pius X represents the first concrete action on the part of the Holy See in favor of the Indians of South America. Aware of, and vitally interested in the rapid development of Latin America, Pius X was concerned with a complete plan of evangelization. At the time, the number of natives and the horrible persecutions to which they were exposed were unknown. When the first reports of the brutal extermination of several Indian tribes of Upper Peru reached the Holy See, the Pope directed his attention particularly to the Putumayo, without, however, losing sight of his primary goal, which was the reorganization of all the missions on the continent.

Father Giovanni Genocchi was chosen by Pius X to investigate the condition of the Indians and the Catholic missions, and to submit a plan of reform. Levi della Vida remarks that "no one was better qualified than Father Genocchi to inform the Pope, and through him world opinion, of the atrocious lot of those unfortunate ones, and of the unspeakable barbarity of their tormentors."[2] Before he had reached

---

[1] Giorgio Levi Della Vida, *Fantasmi ritrovati* (Venezia: Neri Pozza. 1966), p. 116.

[2] *Ibid.*, p. 116. Giovanni Genocchi (1860-1926), was ordained a priest in 1883 and entered the Congregation of the Missionaries of the Sacred Heart. He was named secretary to the Apostolic Delegate of Syria (1886-1888) and Vicar General in Constantinople (1888-1902). From 1892 to 1896 he served on the mission in New Guinea. Upon his return to Italy, Genocchi was permanently stationed in Rome. In August, 1897, Pope Leo XIII conferred on him the chair of Sacred Scripture at the Apollinare University. In May, 1903, Fr. Genocchi was chosen to serve on the Pontifical Biblical Commission. He gave the Greek and Hebrew examinations administered by the Commission for the doctoral degree. His command of biblical and modern languages, plus his understanding of the principles of biblical science quickly earned Giovanni Genocchi a reputation in the field of historical and biblical criticism. In 1902, with the

his thirtieth year, Genocchi had already calmly braved the marsh-fevers of New Guinea. Hence, at fifty, he did not hesitate to expose himself to the risk of yellow fever of the Amazon River and, to what was perhaps the greater impending danger, that posed by men.

Pius X knew Genocchi and esteemed him as "a good priest and an exemplary religious."[3] He could rely completely upon Genocchi's obedience and devotion to the Church. When called to the Secretariate of State to be informed about the mission that the Pope was entrusting to him, Genocchi answered "immediately, even before the matter was explained [to him], that his work, and he himself were, of course, at the service of the Holy See."[4] Genocchi confided to Cardinal Andrea Ferrari: "I was even happier when I learned that the matter concerned a work truly worthy of the Church of Jesus Christ." He added with

---

collaboration of Fr. Giovanni Semeria and Fr. Giuseppe Clementi, Fr. Genocchi realized one of his best undertakings: the first Italian modern translation of the Gospels. The success was enormous: in the first six months one-hundred and fifty thousand copies were sold and by 1950 the total reached twenty million. Although the aim of the publication was pastoral and ecumenical, the footnotes, written by Genocchi, aroused the admiration of Biblical specialists. Msgr. Edward J. Hanna, Archbishop of San Francisco, related the following comment of an American scriptural scholar: "I have never seen work of this kind done in such a way; here one has the last word of science rendered with childlike simplicity."

During the modernist crisis he was bitterly attacked and accused of having introduced modernism in Rome. However, his correspondence with the modernists clearly shows how unfounded these charges were. His writings have not the slightest trace of modernism. Pius X, as intent on stopping the heresy as he was, when confronted by these charges against Genocchi, took up his defense. On February 1, 1920, Pope Benedict XV named Genocchi Apostolic Visitor to the Ukraine, and, at the end of January 1923, Pius XI made him Apostolic Visitor to the dioceses of Lwow, Stalislaviv and Przemsyl.

Father Genocchi was commonly recognized as a man of superior intelligence and moral integrity. Bishop Angelo Roncalli, the future Pope John XXIII, after acclaiming Father Genocchi "a truly remarkable man in the Church of the Lord... an absolute gentleman, that is to say, a noble soul, a soul truly permeated with the spirit of the Gospel," wrote: "One day he invited me to dinner and favored me with two or three conversations which left me deeply edified. ... His was a very difficult form of holiness; therefore, that much more meritorious and worthy of admiration. He was a source of comfort for all candid souls seeking the truth, the Holy Church and the triumph of Christ. Above all, Father Genocchi was always devoted to the Sacred Heart and to Our Lady (oh, how much he edifies me). He grew more each day in the serene and gentle light of the spiritual direction of St. Francis de Sales." (AGG. L. 15/R).

See Vincenzo Ceresi, *Padre Genocchi* (Tipografia Poliglotta Vaticana, 1934); Francesco Turvasi, *Giovanni Genocchi e la controversia modernista* (Roma: Ed. Storia e Letteratura, 1974).

[3] Pius X to G. Genocchi, December 28, 1907. AGG. L.15/P.

[4] G. Genocchi to Cardinal A. Ferrari, August 26, 1911. Archives of the Diocese of Milan (Italy).

candor: "If I hold that one may in the proper way question ecclesiastical administration and even protest against it, I also hold firmly that one must never refuse Jesus Christ or one who can speak in his name the sacrifice of one's preference, and even one's own life." [5] When, from his mission post, he was in danger of falling victim to yellow fever, Genocchi wrote: "I am content to suffer, for I do so in order to obey Our Lord, and the Holy Father which is one and the same thing.... Were I to die in carrying out this assignment or any other given to me by the Holy See, I should be happy simply to have done my duty towards Jesus Christ." [6]

---

[5] *Ibid.*
[6] G. Genocchi to T. Mantrici, March 4, 1912. AGG. L.11/M.

INTRODUCTION

The grave and difficult mission entrusted to Genocchi was to include all of South America, but particularly the Putumayo. The region called the Putumayo, or Iça, consists of the area drained by two tributaries of the Putumayo River, the Igaraparaná and the Caraparaná. These two rivers originate near the watershed of the Japura, itself a tributary of the Amazon river, further east. They run parallel in a southwesterly direction for some 300 or 400 miles and end in the Putumayo before the junction of the Putumayo with the Amazon River. The region is approximately 10,000 square miles. It is situated between the equator and the second degree of south latitude and between the seventy-second and seventy-fourth degree of west longitude. The Igaraparaná is navigable for a vessel of 100 tons to a point 220 miles from its mouth, where the city La Chorrera is located. The most important city on the Caraparaná is El Elcanto, near the junction of the Putumayo River.

At the beginning of the twentieth century this region was bordered on the west by Ecuador, on the north by Colombia, on the south by Peru, and on the east by Brazil. It was disputed territory, claimed by Peru and Colombia. Today the region belongs to Colombia and the Putumayo River, a 980 miles long tributary of the Amazon River, forms the southern boundary of Colombia with Ecuador and Peru.

It does not seem likely that, in the years before the arrival of Genocchi, missions or missionaries had penetrated the regions in question. Except for raids of slave traders, the contact of the natives with white men was a tale of a distant and far-off past. When Genocchi arrived in the Putumayo, there were no more than 10,000 Indians. He records in his notes that just six years earlier, in 1906, according to the French explorer, Eugenio Rabuchon, the Indian population had reached 50,000.[1] The four main tribes, which once belonged to the ancient empire of the Incas, were the Huitotos, the Boras, the Andokes, and the

---

[1] Eugenio Rabuchon, *En el Putumayo y sus Afluentes* (Lima, 1907). E. Rabuchon was a French explorer, who lost his life travelling in the Putumayo. His book was an official publication in Spanish, the Peruvian Minister of Foreign Affairs having instructed the Peruvian Consul General to edit Rabuchon's diary. The publication was made at the cost of the Peruvian government.

Ocainas. Of the smaller tribes, the Recigaros and the Muinames were most frequently mentioned. The Huitoto tribe was probably the largest and may have reached a population of 30,000 at one time. Regarding their civilization, Genocchi recounts that prisoners taken in wars were more than likely eaten. The Amazon cannibals, however, do not seem to have killed to eat, as is the case with many primitive races, but in many instances they did eat those they killed. The victims were not terrified at the prospect of being eaten, and in some cases, they regarded it as an honorable end. Genocchi quoted Lieutenant Robert Maw, who related the case of a girl on the Brazilian Amazon in 1827 who actually preferred to be eaten by her own kind rather than become a slave of a Portuguese trader.[2]

The history of the evangelization of the Indians of the Putumayo goes back to 1610, when the first Reduction in the district of Loreto, to which the Putumayo belonged, was formally established.[3] Fifty years prior to that, the district was frequented by Jesuit missionaries. Under the jurisdiction of the bishops of Peru, they established many Christian settlements among Indians. One member of the Society, Father José de Anchieta, known as the Xavier of South America, soon became known as the Apostle and *Thaumaturgus* [miracle maker]. A companion of his missionary travels, Father Thomas Fields, had been sent to Tucuman and Paraguay in 1587. He was apparently the first to learn the languages of all the Indian tribes of Paraguay.

Father Fields was sometimes accompanied by two other priests, Francisco Solano and Manuel de Ortega. They converted 10,000 Indian cannibals and rescued many of their prisoners who were being fattened

---

[2] Robert Maw was an officer of the British Navy who crossed the continent from the Pacific to the Atlantic, by way of the Amazon early in the last century.

[3] The Reductions were Indian villages from which European settlers were excluded. They were located near a river and were grouped around a plaza. On one side were the church, the priests' house, a home for widows and orphans, the cemetery, storehouses and offices. The other three sides were made up of Indian homes. In each reduction there were the pastor and at least one other priest. Agriculture was a communal project. Domestic industries were encouraged and their products as well as agricultural surpluses were sold by the missionaries to procure any items needed in the mission economy. The Indians were taught Christian doctrine, reading and writing. Their native abilities in painting and sculpture were encouraged and used in the decorating of the churches. All work was tied in with communal religious prayers (H. Storni, *New Catholic Encyclopedia* [New York, 1967] vol. XII, p. 166).

See Ludovico Muratori, *Relation of the Mission of Paraguay* (London: printed for J. Marmaduke in Long-Acre, 1759); Cunninghame Graham, *A Vanished Arcadia* (1901); Philip Caraman, *The Lost Paradise* (New York: Seabury Press, 1976). For a brief history of the reduction in the district of Loreto (Peru), see *America*, August 3, 1912, p. 389-390.

for consumption. In every place the missionaries evangelized, they erected a church with the help of their converts and began to civilize the Indians. This gave rise to the Reduction. In 1605 Father Fields was joined by Fathers José Cataldino and Simon Maceta and later on by Father Diego Torres, the Provincial, and fifteen others. Because they fell prey to calumny for refusing to lend themselves to the exploitation or enslavement of the Indians, Father Pablo Valdivio went to Madrid to obtain authority from the king to protect and isolate the Indians. In 1608, Philip III issued letters supporting the Society of Jesus for their work of evangelization of the Indians. Thus, in 1610, the Reduction of Loreto was established with the consent of the Spanish government which approved the exclusion of Europeans.

The communal life established in the Reduction, where the Indians wandering in the vicinity were gathered together, had the church as its focal point. The missionaries had much to endure from the so-called *mamelucos*, hordes of mestizos from the Brazilian colony, who conducted vast scale slave hunts. The missionaries finally armed their Indians, and in 1641, inflicted a decisive defeat on the mamelucos. Under the patriarchal leadership of the missionaries, the Indians were educated with great success in the Christian and civilized way of life, and thrived with their orchards, herds, and well-stored granaries. This prosperity, however, proved to be the downfall of the mission. The more the missions prospered the more the stories spread that there was gold and wealth in those inaccessible Jesuit missions. With the expulsion of the Jesuits in 1767, the Reductions collapsed and the Indians were forced to return to the forests.

CHAPTER I

A PONTIFICAL STUDY MISSION

Between May 22 and June 7, 1911, the Apostolic Delegates of
Peru, Bolivia, Colombia, Costa Rica and Mexico, and the Internuncios
of Chile and Argentina received a circular letter from the Secretary of
State, Cardinal Merry del Val. The letter read:

> Your Excellency is not unaware of the sad state in which many
> indigenous populations in the vast central territories of Latin America
> find themselves. They are still without the light of the Gospel despite
> the many provisions which have been made and are still being made for
> the growth and the expansion of the Church in these republics. The
> unhappy condition of so many souls immersed in the shadows of
> ignorance and error cannot fail to make a keen impression on the Holy
> Father. He is planning to have the Pontifical representatives in Latin
> America direct their study and their concern to so very serious a
> subject. In order, therefore, to place the Holy See in a position to take
> useful measures to achieve the aim of providing, in as much as is
> possible, the benefit of the true faith for those souls, by the order of
> His Holiness I call upon your Excellency to gather all available facts
> and information concerning this important question, and to write up a
> thorough report of it for the Holy See.[1]

The pontifical representatives were to make a report on what
had already been achieved by the missions among the Indians within
the boundaries of their delegations, noting the number and the
importance of the missionary institutes which existed in them. News
which had reached the Congregation for the Propagation of the Faith
and the Secretary of State prompted Pius X to ask all the Pontifical
representatives in South America for precise information on the
condition of the Indians along the entire continent. On October 4,
1909, Father Agostino Alemany, the Prefect Apostolic of San
Francisco of the Ucayali, in his annual report to the Congregation
for the Propagation of the Faith, denounced the "iniquitous

---

[1] ASV.SS. F.4. 9.

treatment to which the rubber merchants subjected the wretched natives," and went on to say:

> The social misfits, the immoral, the criminals of every nation, and even the Jews, are pouring in here in great numbers. A general state of immorality and specific crimes frustate any effort at preaching Christian morals and faith. A total lack of shame has led to the horrible state of affairs in which the laws of marriage and society contribute to the vicious and appalling way married and unmarried women are treated. Add to all this the horrible practice of going out in war parties to hunt down unarmed native forest dwellers. The inevitable consequences of this practice are: the death of the native heathens, captivity for the women and children, their exile forever along with unspeakable suffering; in a word, a bloody business that should be wiped out for many reasons. Some businessmen along these rivers get control of tracts in the middle of nowhere and in a few years come out rich, some even very wealthy. They are able to do this through the work of thirty, forty or more families of native heathens whom they have reduced to a state of degraded slavery. They also buy them and then sell them off separately with all the painful and pitiable separations and departures this entails. Only a few days ago I witnessed how the buying and selling of two native heathen girls was carried out for the ridiculous price of forty shekels. We witnessed the weeping and lamentation of the girls as they were violently separated from their friends. A Jewish man bought them. Where did he take them? As can be seen by anyone, this moral perversion, along with the criminal commerce, places serious obstacles in the way of the missionaries' zeal and the conversion of the heathens.[2]

The following year, on October 4, the same Prefect Apostolic, Father Alemany, reported:

> Since the middle of the last century the extraction of rubber has flourished as a business especially in Peru. As a result the number of the civilized people is growing more and more and they have set their mind and heart on whatever business is of importance to European trade. But the business of extracting rubber offers little hope for profit unless the native heathens who know the terrain perfectly are used in the operation. Those interested in the extraction of rubber will not go into the business unless they have what they consider to be a sufficient number of heathen natives. They buy them from other colonists who consider it perfectly legitimate to buy and sell the natives, although in doing this they act unjustly. Nevertheless, the rubber extractor sends representatives into the heathens' area where they attack with their battle gear, burn the homes or make sure they are destroyed. They seize the defenseless

---

[2] A. Alemany to Cardinal G. Gotti, October 4, 1909. ACPF. R.151. 2438.

women and children, kill the old, and fight the men who struggle to defend themselves, their families and the land they don't want to leave. But the men are either slaughtered or dragged off to the place where they will work at extracting rubber. They will do this for many years under the most severe vigilance and rigorous discipline. Often the whole course of their natural life will be spent in collecting, distributing, carrying and transporting the aforementioned commodity from place to place." [3]

Several times the Holy See appealed to the Peruvian government to take steps to bring an end to these atrocities against the Indians. When he received the reports of Father Alemany, Cardinal Merry del Val immediately informed Msgr. David Quattrocchi, Chargé d'Affaires in Peru, with the information. He was directed to call the government's attention "to the deplorable facts, invoking provisions to suppress abuses no less contrary to religion than deplorable to dignity and to the prestige of Peru." The Foreign Minister, Mr. Porras, welcomed the solicitude of the Holy See, and let them know of his appreciation. He took the instructions and directives of the case to the authorities. Porras added, however, that the mistreatment of the Indians and the difficulty of changing their situation were partly due to the fact of international disputes over the boundaries of the territory. In the course of such disputes none of the governments concerned exercised the direct intervention or the vigilance which was necessary in the disputed territories. The effects of the vigilance would be felt soon afterwards when such problems had been resolved, as for example in the territory which had been the object of controversy between Peru, Bolivia, and Brazil. [4]

The Peruvian government settled nothing, aside from sending Judge Romulo Paredes who carried out a serious investigation and reached the conclusion that approximately three hundred persons should be arrested and condemned. Until then, however, he had not succeeded in putting even ten criminals behind bars. In the meantime, "all of the others, of whom the three hundred mentioned are only a

---

[3] A. Alemany to Cardinal G. Gotti, October 4, 1910. ACPF. R.151. 299.

[4] Cardinal R. Merry del Val to G. Genocchi, July 15, 1911. ASV.SS. 51712. On June 28, 1911, the British Consul at Lima, Lucien J. Jerome reported to the Foreign Office a conversation he had with Msgr. Quattrocchi, the Chargé d'Affaires of the Holy See: "Incidentally I spoke of the crimes committed on the Putumayo.... He informed me for the first time that the Holy See had made over a year ago strong representations to the Peruvian Government, with a view to measures being taken to stop the crimes perpetrated by the *caucheros* [rubber traders] on the Indians in the Amazon region." PRO.FO. 31084.

small fraction, continue their trade in human flesh, undisturbed and triumphant." Msgr. Quattrocchi, who communicated this information to the Secretary of State, added the following detail. "In a festival given by the members of an English rubber company, one of the events on the program consisted of target shooting with fifty natives as the targets. These natives, running up a hill, were shot to death by the revellers, who were drunk with whiskey and champagne." Msgr. Quattrocchi concluded: "As a matter of fact, I could cite horrors of this kind, or worse, by the thousand." [5]

* * *

Two or three weeks after Cardinal Merry del Val's circular letter was sent, further alarming news on the condition of the Indians reached the Holy See. What had been occurring in the Ucayali was being repeated in a far more ferocious manner in the Putumayo. Following the denunciation by an American Engineer, William E. Hardenburg, who had named British subjects in his exposé, the English government had sent a commission of inquiry into the Putumayo, headed by Roger Casement. [6] In two reports sent to Sir Edward Grey on March 17 and

---

[5] Msgr. D. Quattrocchi to Cardinal R. Merry del Val, August 23, 1911. ASV.SS. F.4. 46-52.

[6] The English paper, *The Truth*, in the issue of September 22, 1909 (p. 664), in an article based on information supplied by W. Hardenburg, made the following indictment:

"As set forth by *La Sancion*, the charges are that the agents of the company 'force' the pacific Indians of the Putumayo to work day and night at the extraction of rubber without the slightest remuneration; that they give them nothing to eat; that they rob them of their crops, their women, and their children, to satisfy the voracity, lasciviousness, and avarice of themselves and their employees, for they live on the Indians' food, keep harems of concubines, and sell these people wholesale and retail in Iquitos; that they flog them inhumanly until their bones are laid bare; that they do not give them any medical treatment, but let them linger, eaten by maggots, till they die, to serve afterwards as food for the chiefs' dogs; that they mutilate them, cut off their ears, fingers, arms, and legs; that they torture them by means of fire, of water, and by tying them up, crucified head down; that they burn and destroy their houses and crops; that they cut them to pieces with *machetes* [hunting knives]; that they grasp children by the feet and dash out their brains against walls and trees; that they have the old folk killed when they can work no longer; finally, that to amuse themselves, to practice shooting, or to celebrate the *sabato de gloria*, as Fonseca and Macedo have done, they discharge their weapons at men, women, and children, or, in preference to this, they souse them with kerosene and set fire to them, to enjoy their desperate agony."

On July 1910 the British Consul Roger Casement was instructed to proceed to the Putumayo, on the grounds that several Barbadian negroes, who were prominent in Hardenburg's list of crimes, were British subjects.

21, 1911, Casement confirmed Hardenburg's accusation of atrocities committed against the Indians, and suggested the establishment of a Catholic mission to prevent a repetition of similar crimes. On June 15, Msgr. Manuel Bidwell, chancellor of the Archdiocese of Westminster, delivered the following Memorandum to the Holy See on behalf of the British government:

> As a result of reports which had come to the knowledge of His Majesty's Government with regard to the treatment of the native Indians in the rubber-growing districts of the Upper Amazon, and more especially in the Putumayo where a British company was involved, one of His Majesty's Consular Officers was appointed to proceed to this district in connection with a commission of inquiry sent out by the above-mentioned company against whom accusations, originating in a certain London periodical, had long been directed.
>
> This officer, on the termination of his mission, submitted in March last an exhaustive report to the Secretary of State. His statements which are borne out by those of the company's commission reveal an appalling state of affairs. The natives who are ostensibly paid for collecting and bringing in the rubber are in reality no better than slaves and are compelled to work under a system of the most inhuman cruelty. They are afflicted with every form of torture possible to devise, and are murdered wholesale at the caprice of their employer. It is estimated that at the present rate the entire native population will have disappeared within the space of a few years.
>
> The Peruvian Government to whom the facts have been communicated have expressed their determination to put an end to this state of affairs, and the British company in question is at present engaged in drawing up a scheme of reform. There are however many obstacles among which are the inaccessibility of the Putumayo and the consequent difficulty of communication with the outside world, and the complete lack of any beneficial or civilizing influences.
>
> The consular officer sent out to the Putumayo expressed it as his personal opinion that much good would result from the establishment of a Roman Catholic Mission, with headquarters at Iquitos or some other convenient centre, which could from time to time send representatives to inquire into the welfare of the natives in the outlying districts and generally watch over their interest, and from inquiries which he made of the Peruvian Authorities in Loreto, he understood them to look with favour on such an idea.[7]

---

[7] ASV.SS. F.4.6. On March 2, 1911, in a letter addressed to Louis Mallet at the Foreign Office Roger Casement wrote:

"We can force the Company in London to carry out any action of reform we choose. Upon that you need have no doubt for their own Commission will be with you. One of the first steps shoulds be the appointment of an Inspector — an English officer

As a consequence of this Memorandum, Cardinal Merry del Val sent a second circular letter to the pontifical representatives. He notified them that the Pope "firmly animated by the most ardent interest in the native people of Latin America" had decided to act immediately, and to send a person competent and experienced in missionary work, Father Giovanni Genocchi, to those republics. He would dedicate all of his activity and his zeal to gathering all the facts and information to which the pontifical representatives' attention and concern had already been called in the previous circular letter. This work would enable Genocchi to inform the Holy See precisely of the facts and to present them with concrete and advantageous proposals for the spiritual welfare of the Indians. The Apostolic Delegates, therefore, "in the interest of the apostolic concern of the Holy Father for those poor unhappy ones and in obedience to his august instructions," would suitably entertain and come to an agreement with Genocchi "about a matter of such great interest for the welfare of the souls." Furthermore, they were to furnish him with all the information and suggestions relating to the case. If

---

preferably to my mind — at a good big salary, and a carefully chosen good man to go out to the Putumayo. They want not merely inspection but administration. Izon will welcome this, and the Prefect in Loreto himself suggested it to me. I told him that the Commission had always determined on the recommendation of an inspector.

Another suggestion that should be supported is the establishment of a Mission in the Putumayo. It would have to be a Catholic Mission for the Lima Government recognizes only the one Church. The Company should be induced to give every facility to the establishment of a Catholic Mission and later on the Lima Government too. I sounded the Prefect on this point too and he was cordially helpful, save as for a Protestant Mission which he said would be a stumbling block. I consider a Mission on the Putumayo will be more effective to save the Indians and improve their lot and prevent crime than any other measure we could take up." PRO.FO. 8012.

Roger Casement (born September 1, 1864, in Sandycove, a suburb of Dublin — died August 3, 1916 in London) was a British consul in Portuguese East Africa (1895-1898), Angola (1898-1900), Congo (1901-1904) and Brasil (1906-1911). He gained international fame for revealing the cruelties committed in the Congo by the white traders against the natives. His report published in 1904 aroused a deep international concern (See *The Cambridge History of Africa*, VI [1870-1905], p. 321-370). In Belgium, after a commission established by King Leopold confirmed Casement's report, polemics blazed between socialists and Belgian Catholics, headed by the Jesuits (in this matter there is abundant documentation in the Jesuit Archives in Rome).

In July 1914, Casement visited America and sought political and financial support for Irish independence. Then, when World War I broke out, he went to Germany to seek help and to recruit an Irish brigade from Irish prisoners. When he landed from a German submarine off the coast of Kerry, he was captured by British police. He was convicted of high treason on June 29, 1916, and hanged in Pentonville on August 3, 1916. By his execution he became a martyr of the Irish revolt against British rule in Ireland.

necessary, they were to put him in contact with the local bishops, supplying him with letters of introduction when suitable, and even putting him in contact with the other authorities and persons who might be useful to him in the execution of his task.[8]

* * *

On July 6, 1911, Genocchi was called to the Secretariate of State, where he was told of his appointment as Apostolic Visitor. Cardinal Merry del Val went on to inform Genocchi of the scope of this mission entrusted to him by the Holy Father. He spoke of the sad plight of the many indigenous peoples in the central territories of Latin America, which continued to exist despite the various measures which had been taken by the Church. The Pope himself, "eager to hasten, as much as possible, the benefit of faith to so many souls," decided to send Father Genocchi to Latin America. His task was to observe and to study in the most appropriate manner, and by the most opportune means, all that related to the existing condition of those natives and to the question of their evangelization.

The mission entrusted to Genocchi had a twofold purpose. His first care was to report to the Holy See on the actual state of the Indians, and on the situation of the missions on the whole continent of South America. He would gather geographical and ethnological information on those territories to which the activities of the dioceses and the missions had not yet extended. He would also report on the number and characteristics of the natives, on their principal centers, on their means of communication, and on the difficulties which might hinder their evangelization. He was to state what, in his opinion, the possible disposition of the government might be in this regard and what cooperation might be expected on the part of the same. Finally, Genocchi, after interrogating persons of authority and expertise, was to communicate to the Holy See "all suggestions which, together with the aforesaid information, and with his opinion in the matter, might serve as a basis for a practical and useful study on the best way to initiate and promote an undertaking of such importance."

His second care, more directly and urgently, was of intervening fully and actively in the problem of the atrocities systematically inflicted by the rubber traders on the Indians of the Putumayo. Genocchi was informed that two facts would help him to start his mission on a firm base. The Holy See, through Msgr. Quattrocchi, had made a diplomatic

---

[8] ASV.SS. F.4. 6.

appeal to the Peruvian government on behalf of the Indians. The government's response was an appreciation of the Holy See's concern for the Indians. In addition, a communication from the English government had reached the Holy See a few days earlier. It confirmed the abuses committed by a British rubber company in the territory of the Putumayo. In the same communication it was stated that the Peruvian government declared itself ready to put an end to such horrors; likewise, the company involved had assumed the obligation of presenting a series of reforms and provisions. Furthermore it was proposed that a Roman Catholic mission be established and the Peruvian authority of Loreto apparently looked favorably on this idea. The most urgent task, Genocchi was told, was to formulate for the Holy See a concrete plan for the ecclesiastical reorganization of Iquitos, the capital of the Putumayo. He was to keep in mind that that city was already the center of the homonymous Prefecture directed by the Augustinian Fathers. For some years then the government had promised to provide a territory in Iquitos itself in which to erect the principal center of all the established missions and those to be established. Genocchi, keeping these projects in mind, had to confer with the Apostolic Delegate. At the same time, he was to study the most concrete and efficacious ways and means by which the Holy See, in agreement with, and possibly aided by the Peruvian government, could "initiate and exercise a charitable action for the relief of those wretched natives in the interests of religion and civilization." [9]

In the days that followed Genocchi had further interviews with the Secretary of State in order to map out his mission. He was to visit first Argentina, then Chile, Peru, Bolivia and other neighboring countries. On July 13 Genocchi was given credentials to present to representatives of the Holy See in South America. They were requested "to welcome and help him as much as possible in carrying out the delicate and difficult task the Holy Father was entrusting to him." [10] Genocchi was granted "complete liberty of movement with full authority and unrestricted financial means." The pontifical representatives were directed to give him "whatever he deemed necessary." [11] On July 15, the Secretary of State delivered written instructions to Genocchi.

On the eve of his departure Genocchi met with the Prefects of those Congregations which were concerned with his mission: Cardinal

---

[9] Cardinal R. Merry del Val to G. Genocchi, July 15, 1912. ASV.SS. F.4 14.

[10] Cardinal R. Merry del Val to the Vatican representatives in South America, July 13, 1911. ASV.SS. F.4. 10.

[11] G. Genocchi to Cardinal A. Ferrari, August 24, 1911. Archives of the diocese of Milan (Italy).

José C. Vives y Tuto, the Prefect of the Congregation for Religious, Cardinal Gaetano De Lai, the Secretary of the Consistorial Congregation, and Cardinal Girolamo Gotti, the Prefect of the Congregation for the Propagation of the Faith. Genocchi met also with Cardinal Mariano Rampolla, the President of the Pontifical Biblical Commission. Though he greatly regretted losing the valuable collaboration of Genocchi, an active member of his commission, Cardinal Rampolla admitted he was "very pleased with the beautiful mission entrusted to Genocchi for which [he had] great hopes." [12]

On July 16, Genocchi had an audience with Pope Pius X. Pius X recognized that, along with the rapid development of Latin America, there must be a complete plan of evangelization. During the audience it was most apparent that the Pope was deeply concerned about the brutal extermination of several Indian tribes in South America and the inability of the missionaries, due to poor organization, to save the souls and bodies of the Indians. The Pope, moved to tears, referred to the Indians as "those poor and persecuted beloved sons." [13] Genocchi later related to Cardinal Alfonso Capecelatro that the Holy Father had bestowed on him many favors and blessings for the mission he was about to undertake. On July 19, 1911, three days after his audience with the Pope, Genocchi left Rome for Genoa where he was to embark on a ship for Buenos Aires.

* * *

In the meantime, Cardinal Merry del Val, in a letter to Bidwell on July 10, sent a reply to the English government. The London prelate put the letter of the Secretary of State in the form of a Memorandum and, on July 12, went to the Foreign Office to deliver it personally to Mr. Dister Drummond. In his Memorandum Bidwell declared:

> The suggestion contained in the Foreign Office Memorandum on the Putumayo question has strengthened the desire of the Vatican Authorities to promote by every means in their power and as energetically as possible the evangelization of the pagan masses in South America. There are undoubtedly millions of natives throughout the South American Republics who are living in complete ignorance of Christianity. The governments do not like to admit this fact which they consider humiliating, but they do not, and indeed cannot, deny it. They are glad that the Church should work to civilize these natives, although they are unwilling in some cases to

---

[12] G. Genocchi to Cardinal A. Capecelatro, July 17, 1911. AGG. L.3/C.
[13] See p. 53.

say so openly for fear of appearing "clerical," and they are disposed to give facilities to Catholic missionaries.

A circular was sent recently from the Vatican to the Papal Delegates in South America, calling their attention to the importance of this work and asking for full information and the best means of dealing with it. With regard to Peru, the Vatican Authorities are informed that it is impossible to reach the natives from Iquitos; and that, for the work to be done effectively, a centre should be established further on. Their information, however, is very incomplete and they are entertaining the idea of sending out a capable official to report.

The chief difficulty in regard to this work is to find the funds required to carry it out. The Vatican is prepared to find missionaries, but means must be found to pay for their passage, for their maintenance, etc. It is not possible for them to depend on the natives as this would hamper their work and arouse hostility on the part of those whom they are called upon to help. Brazil has a "Civilization Fund" from which some help is given to missionaries, but it does not appear that the Peruvian Government is disposed at present to furnish means for the establishment of a Mission. If the British Government could bring pressure to bear on the Government of Peru to provide a fund and to take up the matter in a proper way with the Holy See, it would be a great advantage.[14]

Bidwell added that he would be grateful if he might be able to state in his letter to the Vatican how the Foreign Office viewed the suggestion that the English government should approach the Peruvian government. He would ask Cardinal Merry del Val if he could give the British government the name of the priest who had been recently traveling in the Putumayo region.

Drummond, after discussing Cardinal Merry del Val's Memorandum with Casement, noted that undoubtedly the establishment and maintenance of the missions in the Putumayo was the best means of protecting the Indians. In view of the fact that the rubber company was almost certain to collapse in the course of a few weeks and that, consequently, the Foreign Office would not be able to work through it, the British government was morally bound to do what it could to help those people in some other way. Drummond was not sure the Foreign Office could ask the Peruvian government officially to provide funds for the maintenance of a Catholic mission. They could not ask the Peruvian government to support a Protestant mission, because Peru, as a Catholic country, might reply that it would not accept a Protestant mission. This would be the response of the British government if they were critized for failing to ask support for a Protestant mission. Casement thought that the best solution was to raise funds in England by a yearly subscription.

---

[14] PRO.FO. 27718.

That same day Casement met with Bidwell and discussed various points about the question of a mission raised by Cardinal Merry del Val. Following the discussion, Bidwell notified the Cardinal that Casement seemed "very anxious indeed that a mission be established as soon as possible," for, as Casement himself had recounted, the atrocities committed by the white people there were beyond description. Casement had succeeded in dispersing the gang of criminals for the time being, and was working to consolidate the good work already accomplished. For this reason he was trying to save the English company that had the contract in the district. Although many of the crimes committed were due to company agents, the director in England had absolutely no knowledge of what was going on. Having been informed, he promised that he would do all he could to prevent things of this kind from occurring again. If the company disappeared the whole district would once more fall into the hands of the Peruvian and Colombian *conquistadores* who were responsible for all of the horrors committed. But, in Casement's opinion, no company would be able to do any real civilizing work. For this reason a mission was necessary, and the Foreign Office was well aware that only a Catholic mission was conceivable.

Casement's idea was that a mission, sufficiently strong and well established, could initiate the work of civilization which would spread its good effects to other districts. This, however, could not be done if the missionaries had to rely on the natives for food or were hampered in their work for lack of means. He seemed to think it quite possible that the Foreign Office could tell the Peruvian government that it had to take steps to secure the establishment of a mission, and that it had to support this mission. Yet Casement had no assurance that this would lead to any permanent result. The Peruvian government, he thought, would probably agree at the time. Nevertheless, however quickly or faithfully they carried out their undertaking, Casement was convinced that, after a few years, and especially after a change of government, they would shirk their responsibilities. Repeated pressure on the part of the Holy See and the Foreign Office would be required in order to make them keep their obligation. For this reason Casement was going to suggest that the mission not be wholly dependent for its support upon the Peruvian administration.

Casement suggested that a petition be sent to Ireland to make this missionary effort, that Irish missionaries be sent, and that an appeal be made for a fund sufficient to endow the mission. Some 10,000 to 15,000 pounds needed to be raised for this purpose, and he felt it could be done. Many people in England would also subscribe, Protestants as well as Catholics, and Casement seemed confident of being able to arrange it. Already he had an offer of 1,000 pounds from one man and 2,500 pounds from another. Casement suggested Irish missionaries because he himself was Irish and felt he could accomplish more in Ireland than elsewhere. He also believed that the idea would appeal to his countrymen.

As for the number of missionaries to be sent, Casement thought that at the outset three would suffice. However, several questions arose because in Iquitos the church, or rather a barn where Mass was said, was served by the secular clergy and there was no mission in the district. First, would the local ecclesiastical authorities have anything to say? And, if the Secretary of State did not see any objection to the plan of getting the money for an endowment, would the Holy Father ask the Irish bishops to start it, or should the appeal be put forth by some laymen, and then be blessed by the Holy Father and supported by the bishops? [15]

Bidwell promised Casement that he would try to find out what the Secretary of State thought of the plan. Cardinal Merry del Val was not able to answer the questions presented by Casement. Through the Apostolic Delegate at Lima he sent Bidwell's letter to Genocchi, and urged him to suggest how to answer the proposal in regard to the Irish missionaries and the amount of money required for the support of a missionary. Cardinal Merry del Val then authorized Bidwell to notify the Foreign Office confidentially of the name of the representative sent by the Holy See, but the Cardinal added that he did not wish this talked about more than was necessary. He suggested that the representatives of the British government and the English company should get in touch with Father Genocchi and work out details with him. Father Genocchi was going to Lima first and would probably proceed from there to the Putumayo district.

Casement, however, suggested that it was not opportune to write to the company about Genocchi's mission. Since Genocchi was going to Lima first, he could not possibly reach the Putumayo for many months because of the great difficulty of communications. Casement said, when the time would come for Genocchi to move from Lima, Mr. Des Graz would no doubt give him the necessary introduction and support for his visit to the Putumayo. In the meantime, the Foreign Office sent the following telegram to its representative in Lima, Mr. Lucien Jerome: "The Vatican is sending Father Genocchi to investigate, and report with a view to establishing a mission in the Putumayo. He will go to Lima in the first place, and you should render him all the assistance you properly can." [16]

---

[15] M. Bidwell to Father [Genocchi?], July 17, 1911, and July 20, 1911. ASV.SS. F.4. 64-69.

[16] PRO.FO. 371, 1202, 27718, 30484.

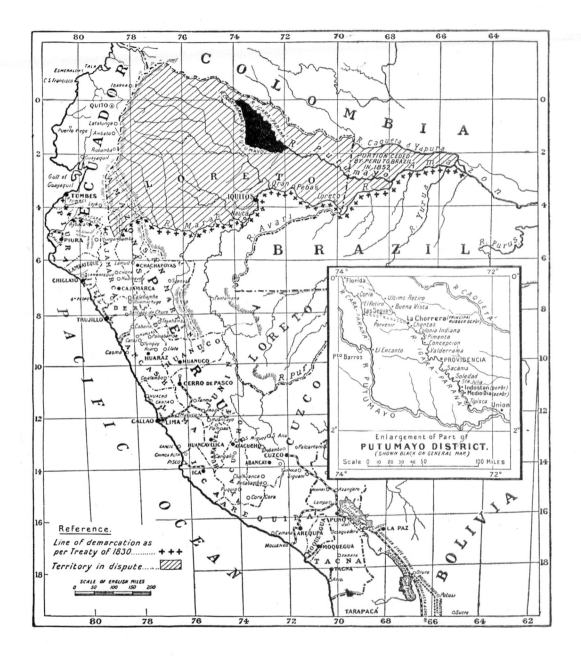

Reference.

Line of demarcation as
per Treaty of 1830............ +++

Territory in dispute........

SCALE OF ENGLISH MILES
0   50   100   150   200

Enlargement of Part of
PUTUMAYO DISTRICT.
(SHOWN BLACK ON GENERAL MAP.)

Scale 0 10 20 30 40 50   100 MILES

CHAPTER II

THE INDIANS OF PATAGONIA, CHAGO, ARAUCANIA, TIERRA DEL FUEGO

On July 20, 1911, Genocchi embarked from Genoa on the *Mafalda* bound for Buenos Aires. After Dakar the ocean became very rough due to the wind from the north. "I did not suffer seasickness," Genocchi wrote, "although the pitching and turning of the ship were very distressing." He could not celebrate Mass or write, so he spent his time reading Spanish books and practicing the language. In a letter written, as he put it, "not far from the coast of Brazil, August 1, 1911," Genocchi informed Cardinal Alfonso Capecelatro (who was to be his special confidant during his mission) of his state of mind. "I feel happy for having consented to the desire of the Pope, as to a desire of Jesus Christ." He went on to say:

> One can disagree with some ideas and with some directions of the Church's government; but a priest and a Catholic religious must not fall short in his obedience and work of service to lawful authority. May God help me in practicing the evangelical virtues.[1]

Genocchi arrived in Buenos Aires the morning of August 5. All the immigrants were transferred to an Argentine steamship ten miles from the port and brought to Martín García, a quarantine island, although health on board was excellent. The Apostolic Internuncio, Msgr. Achille Locatelli, welcomed Genocchi with great courtesy and cordiality. Because he did not have room in his home, the Internuncio asked the Salesians to grant hospitality to the Apostolic Visitor. "This decision pleased me very much," Genocchi informed Cardinal Merry del Val, "because there are missionaries here who have lived among the natives in Patagonia." Genocchi began to collect useful information from many of the missionaries. He also planned to contact the Franciscans who worked in the difficult mission of Chaco in Northern Argentina. At the same time he had an opportunity to practice the Spanish language. It was winter in South America, and consequently it

---

[1] G. Genocchi to Cardinal A. Capecelatro, August 1, 1911. AGG. L.3/C.

was not easy to cross the Andes in the direction of Chile and Peru, for the railroad was blocked by snow. Genocchi thought he would have to spend two or three weeks in Buenos Aires. "However, I am not wasting my time," he assured the Secretary of State, "indeed, I am gathering precious material." Genocchi concluded his letter with this postscript: "May I ask Your Eminence to offer my greetings and best wishes to the Holy Father for the propitious anniversary of his coronation which we shall celebrate here tomorrow with great solemnity." [2]

How conscientiously the trusted emissary of Pius X fulfilled his mission is proven by the large amount of relevant literature Genocchi gathered then in order to understand the situation confronting him. The notebook which Genocchi kept at this time is filled from beginning to end with exercises in the Spanish and Portuguese languages. It is clearly worn from use during his long journeys or during periods of compulsory and enervating inactivity throughout his mission. Along with the notebook are pamphlets and newspapers of all kinds which Genocchi collected. He filled all of his spare moments going through these, with pen in one hand and scissors in the other, arranging everything in order to promote his work and to provide a documentation for his reports to the Secretary of State. During these months nothing seemed to occupy his mind and his heart except the cause of the Indians of South America, their history, the cruelty of the whites towards them and the problem of slavery in general.

The first note about the Indians which we find among his papers is the following passage from the book, *Notes de voyage dans l'Amerique du Sud*, by Georges Clemenceau:

> The Indian of South America, though closely akin to the redskin of the North, is infinitely his superior. He had, indeed, created a form of civilisation, which the *conquistadores* put brutally to an end. There still subsist in the northern provinces of the Argentine some fairly large native settlements which receive but scant consideration from the Government. I heard too much on the subject to doubt the truth of this. Not but what many savage deeds can be laid to the charge of the Indians, as, for example, the abominable trap they laid for the peaceful Crevaux Mission in Bolivia which led to the massacre of all its members. Still, in equity we must remember that those who have recourse to the final argument of brute force are helping to confirm the savages in the habit of using it. In the interest of the higher sentimentality we must all deplore this. But our implacable civilisation has passed sentence on all

---

[2] G. Genocchi to Cardinal R. Merry del Val, August 8, 1911. ASV.SS. F.4, 36-37. Msgr. Achille Locatelli was Apostolic Internuncio to Argentine, 1906-1915.

races that are unable to adapt themselves to our form of social evolution, and from that verdict there is no appeal.

Not that the native of the South is incapable, like his brother of the North, of performing a daily task. I saw many natives amongst the hands employed by M. Hilleret in his factories in Tucuman. Neither can it be said that there is any lack of intelligence in the Indian. But the fact remains that he finds a difficulty in bending the faculties which have grown rigid in the circle of a primitive state of existence to the better forms of our own daily work, and this renders it impossible for him to carve out a place for himself in the sunlight under the new social organism imported from Europe by the white men. With greater power of resistance than the redskins of the other continent, he, like them, is doomed to disappear. Yet in one respect he has been more fortunate than his kinsmen of the North, and will never entirely die out, for he has already inoculated with his blood the flesh of the victors.[3]

The following notes about the first colonizers of Argentina were transcribed by Genocchi in telegraphic style:

† 1537, Pedro De Mendoza, first Governor of Argentina (Granada, Naples and Milan, Sack of Rome).

1536, Juan de Ayolas in Paraguay made a treaty with the Indians who undertook to give Ayolas seven girls and each soldier two girls.

1542, Adelantado Don Alvaro Muñez Babeza de Vaca tried to correct those dissolute customs of the colony by forbidding the soldiers to have more than one woman and taking the land of a great number in punishment for mistreating the Indians. The soldiers formed a conspiracy and shipped Don Alvaro Muñez back to Spain by brute force, where it was hard for him to prove his innocence and to be integrated in his government.

1737, Domingo De Irala signed another treaty with Guaranis, *ut supra*. He took the seven daughters of the chief. This event was considered so normal that Irala in his testament, which has been preserved, asks that his children, whom he had with the seven women, be considered as Spanish.[4]

Another page was filled with the descriptions of the brutality of General José de Urquiza, "a powerful and avaricious storekeeper at Entre Rios." He had been appointed Governor of the provinces Entre

[3] Georges Clemenceau, *Notes de voyage dans l'Amerique du Sud; Argentine, Uraguay, Bresil* (Paris: Hachette, 1911), p. 99-100.

Our quotation is taken from the English translation of G. Clemenccau's book, *South America to-day; a study of conditions, social, political and commercial in Argentina, Uraguay, Brazil* (New York: G. P. Putman's sons, 1911), p. 145-147.

[4] AGG. S. 7/16. See Mesa y Leompart, *Compendio de historia de América* (1902), Vol. I, p. 399, 404.

Rios and Corrientes (1846-1850) at the time of the dictatorship of Juan
Manuel de Rosas in Buenos Aires.

> The soldiers were called up to fight the Unitarists of Corrientes. The
> *gauchos* [cowboys] of the Mocoreto River banks did not respond to the
> call. When the war ended, Urquiza sent men to find these deserters.
> Unable to find them, Urquiza gave orders that their families, old people,
> women and children be seized and sent to a hill which he could see from
> the door of his cottage. In winter Urquiza did not allow them even a
> blanket to keep warm. As food he ordered that they be given legs, guts
> and other parts of dead animals which the gauchos would not eat or the
> blue and deteriorated meat of animals who died of exhaustion. The
> guards took them once a day like a herd of cattle to drink at a creek
> nearby, called Cala. An old man was shot because he tried to talk to the
> general (the guards had been ordered not to talk to the prisoners). At the
> end of the month Urquiza allowed the black soldiers and only the black,
> to choose their women from among the white prisoners (like slaves). At
> the beginning of the summer Urquiza released the prisoners. They
> remained only forty out of 300.... None of the federal officers showed
> such cruelty with the conquered.[5]

Among Genocchi's notes from his historical readings of that time
there is a dreadful page taken from a book by Herbert Ward, *A Voice
from the Congo*. It records the deep indignation of the British House of
Lords when, on February 24, 1908, Lord Cromer stated: "There has
been a cynical disregard of the native races and a merciless exploitation
of the country, in the interest of foreigners, for which I believe a
parallel cannot be found in the history of modern times."[6] After
questioning these last words, "a parallel cannot be found in the history
of modern times" and probably thinking of the conditions of the
American Indians, Genocchi copied the following passages from *A
Voice from the Congo*:

> I have personally witnessed convoys of slaves that had been bought or
> captured being conveyed to tribes who purchase them as food, giving
> ivory in exchange. ... Upon reaching their destination the captives were,
> in most cases, subject to further ordeals, being exchanged into other
> hands until eventually, after having been deliberately fattened, they met
> their tragic fate and their bodies were consumed [p. 277, 279].
> In cases where a suspicion was entertained of an individual captive's
> intention to escape, the unfortunate creature was doomed to lie hobbled

---

[5] AGG. S. 7/13. See Mesa y Leompart, *Op. Cit.*, Vol. II, p. 487 f. José de Urquiza
became the first President of the Argentina confederation from 1853 to 1860. He was
killed in 1871.

[6] Herbert Ward, *A Voice from the Congo* (London: W. Heinemann, 1910), p. 287.

with one foot forced through a hole cut in the section of a log, with a spear-head driven into the wood close beside the limb, rendering it impossible to move except at the risk of laceration. Other means to ensure the prisoner's safe custody consisted in binding both hands above the head to the kingpost of a hut, or binding the arms and plaiting the hair into a braid, which was made fast to a branch overhead [p. 279].

Incredible as it may appear, the statement remains justified by abundant proof, as well as from personal observation, that captives were led from place to place in order that individuals might have the opportunity of indicating, by external marks on the body, the portion they desired to acquire [p. 279-280].

Attached to stakes, immersed to their chins in water, we found four Lulungu captives in a pitiable plight. Following the habit of the country, their captors had subjected these poor captives to a process of soaking preparatory to their being killed and eaten" [p. 282].

Ward had been a guest of Tippo Tib, whose real name was Hamad bin Mohamed. Tib was considered the most prominent of all Arabs engaged in the Central African slave-raiding. His slave-raidings in the country to the west of Nyangwe went on from 1877 to 1897. Ward remembered him as "benevolent in appearance and gentle in his manners ... courteous and dignified." Genocchi cited this comment:

> How incongruous it all was, that Arabs, who persecuted and butchered the natives without the slightest sentiment of mercy, were all earnestly devout in their religious observances! I was always impressed by the scrupulous personal cleanliness of the Arab leaders; their regard for appearances contrasted so strangely with the surroundings.... A well-known saying among Tippo Tib's Arabs was: 'The gun is the king of Africa'. [p. 62, 68].

About this time Genocchi came upon some readings which relieved him in part from the burden of these atrocities. They also served to provide an intensely Christian perspective on the problem of slavery in South America. The reading was a life of St. Peter Claver in Spanish by J. Fernandez.[7] Genocchi copied out in his notes some passages which provided magnificent examples of the Saint's compassionate charity towards the sick, even those with the most repugnant diseases. From 1616 on, St. Peter Claver was active in the port city of Cartagena as an apostle of the whites and especially of the negroes who were brought there and then distributed in the interior. With touching devotion Peter Claver took care of them until his death in 1654.

---

[7] José Fernandez, S.J., *Vida de San Pedro Claver, Apostol de los negros* (Barcelona: Imprenta y Librería de V.E.H. de Subirana, 1888).

Thinking of his own experience of evangelization in New Guinea, Genocchi copied the following quotation from the review *España y América*.[8] Genocchi's selection of the passage betrays in him an urgent sense of need to relieve the poor slaves of their burden, and to promote their moral and social state according to the spirit of Christianity:

> In accordance with the instruction which the twelve Augustinians of Lima received from their Father Provincial, churches have been built, altars erected, and music taught. Efforts have been made for the social welfare of the Indians, whilst the children's affection has been won by love and piety. For to make them children of the Gospel, it was necessary to treat them first as **if they were their children by nature** [Genocchi's emphasis].... In this way the difference between the conduct of the missionaries towards them and that of the Spaniards was brought home to the Indians.[9]

* * *

On August 24 Genocchi left Buenos Aires by train for Mendoza, at the foot of the Andes, where he remained three days. The trip had all the conveniences of the great European lines. During his long journey, Genocchi could observe the vast expanse of the Argentine *pampas*. He wrote, "one sees almost nothing but the *pampas* perfectly flat and uniform as a calm sea, with countless cows, sheep, and horses peacefully intent on eating that never-ending field of grass." Here and there Genocchi saw shanties or huts of mud and zinc-plated iron, flocks of ostriches, numerous small sparrows fluttering and rabbits hopping. The rapid multiplication of these two species of ravenous animals was so great that the Americans cursed the Europeans who first brought them over.

The *pampas* were one of the great riches of the country. Herds multiplied and slept in the open without needing attention. Each landowner surrounded his part of the pampas with stakes and wires, built wells for water, and kept a few shepherds. If dry weather did not kill too many thousands of heads of cattle, he reaped a large gain in a short time. "There will come a day," Genocchi commented, "when the *pampas* divided into small estates, planted with trees which attract the rain, will be able to feed millions of families who will no longer find place in Europe and Asia." His concern, however, was for the Indians.

---

[8] G. Genocchi spent four years (1893-1896) in New Guinea as a missionary. See V. Ceresi, *Op. Cit.*, p. 174-267.

[9] AGG. S. 7/15. See *España y América*, 2 (1904), p. 258, 382. The quotation is a part of a letter written by Fr. Colancha.

"Once the Indian tribes wandered through the *pampas* in search of game. Now they are no longer there, and the last survivors are refugees elsewhere for fear of the merciless Europeans, who seized their land, oppressing the old owners with rifleshot."

At 7:00 a.m. on August 25 Genocchi arrived in Mendoza. It reminded him of the Italian city of Messina. In 1861, on the evening of March 20 at 8:30 p.m., Mendoza experienced the terrible fate of Messina. There beneath the ruins of the earthquake some 6,000 people, almost the total population, died. It was rebuilt for the most part with small houses, one-storied buildings. In 1911 Mendoza had 50,000 inhabitants. For many miles, the area was surrounded with pleasant vineyards which did extraordinarily well under what was usually a clear sky. There were very few rainy days. One might even say that in Mendoza it never rained, so rarely did it occur. The nocturnal dew gave the necessary moisture to the land and the sun continually enlarged and ripened the rich clusters of grapes. Genocchi noted, "Some settlers who came here a few years ago with a few thousand Italian lire are already millionaires. Other families, who were in bleak poverty obtained on credit a little plot of land and now live in comfort." The country was populated with Italians whose sons already took pride in calling themselves Argentines and knew only Spanish. They understood the language of their parents, but they no longer spoke it. From what Genocchi was able to see and hear, two-thirds of the Argentine population were either Italian or sons of Italians. The Salesians accomplished great good for the Italians throughout Argentina with their numerous institutes of arts and trades and with their schools.

Genocchi visited the local shrine of Our Lady where General José de San Martino, the chief author of South American independence, had dedicated his Command staff in 1818. Genocchi wrote down the General's letter of dedication:

Mendoza, August 12, 1818.

Reverend Father Guardian of the Monastery of Saint Francis of the City of Mendoza!
The sound protection which its patron and supreme commander, Our Lady of Mount Carmel has lent to the army of the Andes is very visible. A sentiment of Christian gratitude spurs me to present to the Virgin, who is venerated in the monastery directed by your Paternity, the present staff as her property and as a badge of the supreme command which she exercises over the said army. May God preserve you for many years!

José de San Martino [10]

---

[10] G. Genocchi, "Da Buenos Aires a Santiago", in *La Buona Novella* (Roma: ed. M.S.C., 1912), p. 48-49.

From Mendoza, Genocchi sent his second report to the Holy See. He informed Cardinal Merry del Val of his movements from Buenos Aires to Mendoza and of his hope of leaving for Santiago in Chile the following day, provided the train could traverse the snow. He planned to go to Valparaiso, and from there by ship to Callao, the port of Lima in Peru. Genocchi derived many benefits from his stay in Argentina, chiefly that of learning the Spanish language, which was indispensable for his mission. In addition to that, he received useful reports on the state of the Indians, and of the missions in Patagónia, in Chaco and in other places beyond the boundaries of Argentina. "With very few exceptions," Genocchi declared, "it is unfortunately true that in Argentina no one wanted to hear about the Indians."

> The people of this nation desire only one thing, that the Indians disappear completely and quickly, which the Argentines mistakenly believe to be fatally inevitable. This is one more reason why the Holy See does well to attend to the matter with haste. In Chaco the Indians are more numerous than in Patagonia, where they perhaps do not number 50,000 among approximately 300,000 inhabitants and they are very much exposed to the oppression of the white people and are therefore more ferocious.[11]

Of all the missions, those of the Salesians in Patagónia were the best conducted. They needed more missionaries, though not many, and greater subsidies, which the government promised but delayed in giving, however much the Internuncio endeavored on his part. The missions of the Franciscans in Chaco "amounted to very little and could scarcely be said to have gotten started at all. They absolutely lacked personnel, not means, if one bore in mind the wealth that the Franciscans displayed in Buenos Aires." Genocchi suggested that by taking fresh and zealous personnel from Europe, they could effectively organize their missions in Chaco without too much difficulty, unless that immense region was divided, and a part of it given to other congregations.

The Internuncio, Msgr. Locatelli, devoted himself to the question of the Indians with diligence. He enjoyed "an excellent reputation in high governmental and civil spheres of Argentina." The ecclesiastics recognized how exemplary his laborious life was. The good lay people appreciated his zeal for Catholic works, knowing that he ably made up for the defect of the bishops in this matter which is beyond their patriarchal habit. Genocchi concluded: "There is so much to be done,

---

[11] G. Genocchi to Cardinal R. Merry del Val, August 27, 1911. ASV.SS. F.4. 40-41.

especially in Buenos Aires, where Christian marriages are relatively few, and immorality, religious indifference, and even aggressive impiety are spreading frighteningly." [12]

On August 28, Genocchi left Mendoza for Santiago, Chile. Mendoza was 2,304 feet above sea level. At 8:15 a.m. he was already in Cacheuta at 3,732 feet above sea level. Genocchi has left this picturesque description of his crossing of the Andes.

> It is not possible to describe the impression that one receives from those gigantic boulders along Rio Mendoza. They protrude with sharp peaks above a frightful gorge or above a pleasant valley to which the train advances by winding its way, and as if in triumph proceeds after having slowly hugged a precipice. From time to time the snow top of Tutpungato, which is 19,614 feet high or that of Acancagua, which is 21,389 feet high, can be seen at a distance.
> Before long we are heading into the midst of the snow. The sun is scorching, and the sky very clear. The wind is not blowing, and during the frequent stops for water we get out to stretch our legs. Snow surrounds us, and yet we do not feel cold. A little beyond Cacheuta is the waterfall of Potrerillos, not very high but as picturesque as can be. At noon we arrive at Zanjon Amarillo at 6,621 feet, and here a third serrated rail begins because the slope becomes steeper. At 1:30 p.m. at 8,123 feet, we arrive at a natural bridge called the Bridge of the Incas. We climb continually until 3:00 p.m., and, at 9,564 feet, arrive at a tunnel of grottoes (*Túnel de la Cuevas*) little more than two miles long, which comes out on the side of Chile. At that height some suffer from mountain sickness because of the rarefaction of the air, and acceleration of the pulse which sends blood rushing to the head and produces a slight dizziness. As for me, if I had not been warned beforehand I do not believe that I would even have noticed it.
> For quite a long time the train runs between two walls of snow, barely high enough to cover the window, and cut in marvellous symmetry. To open the road the snowplow had passed a little before us. Then we saw it at rest, with a line of freight cars. Coming out of the tunnel we find the landscape less frightening and the temperature more pleasant. The pacific seacoast is not so far away, and the people already feel the effects. The train comes down on the three rails, the cogs of the middle one and the powerful brakes checking the speed, which at times is so fast as to make the more timid fear a fatal loss of brakes. About sunset, when in Italy night has already descended (almost five hours' difference), we smell the scent of the almond and peach blossoms which cheer up the green countryside. In Chile spring is beginning.
> The train continues along the road more speedily, and at the mouth of Río Blanco the rack-rail stops. The sun is hidden in the ocean towards

---

[12] *Ibid.*

Australia and the magnificent starlit sky already shows its bright Cross of the South which brings to mind so much history and fills the soul with love and hope. At 10:30 p.m. we arrive at Santiago. I have already had dinner and said my prayers on the train, and I go immediately to bed. I sleep so deeply that the next morning I am amazed to hear about two small earthquakes at different hours of the night.[13]

* * *

In his third report to the Holy See, Genocchi sent news of the Indians and of the missions of Chile: "For today I shall be satisfied to refer to what I have learned and seen in eight days in Chile with Msgr. [Enrico] Sibillia [the Apostolic Internuncio], an old schoolfellow who treated me with an affection which I should almost call enthusiastic." According to Genocchi, in the mountainous region of Chile there was no lack of more or less savage Indians. In addition to hatred of whites and drunkenness, in Araucania there was widespread poligamy. The Araucani were then restricted to a few forests. In the area of the Strait of Magellan, and in the Tierra del Fuego, the western part of which belonged to Chile, the nomadic tribes of Indians had been greatly reduced:

> We are not far from the time in which one pound was paid per male Indian head and five shillings per female head. The captain of the English ship which brought me to Callao and continually travels around South America (Callao-Liverpool), assured me that for the past ten years or so he had not seen a single pirogue of Indians in the strait of Magellan, while previously he had encountered several. It is stated as a fact that the Chilean soldiers for fun used to fire rifle shots at the Indians whom they caught by chance in the countryside. Very soon nothing but a historical memory will remain of the poor race down there.[14]

The German Capuchins, who had their principal center in Valdivia, attended well to the Araucani, while the Salesians cared for the nomadic tribes of the Magellan territory. As for the other Indians, who were scattered everywhere in Chile, "little had been done for want of missionaries in opportune places." The Internuncio had asked for exact information from the heads of the existing missions, but none had yet come.

At Santiago the Pontifical Visitor found the Assumptionist Fathers. He had first met these missionaries in 1889 in the Middle East.

---

[13] G. Genocchi, *Art. Cit.*, p. 49-50.
[14] G. Genocchi to Cardinal R. Merry del Val, September 17, 1911. ASV.SS. F.4. 56-57. Msgr. Enrico Sibilia was Apostolic Internuncio to Chile, 1908-1914.

He was happy to find among them an old acquaintance from Constantinople, Father Anton Maubon, but was happier still to be able to praise the zeal and spirit of obedience and sacrifice of these priests. With pleasure Genocchi heard from Father Maubon that they would be disposed to accept a mission among the Indians if the Holy See should ask. Genocchi could not help admiring what he termed "their zeal and spirit of obedience and sacrifice *usque ad mortem.*" They were so well trained in their spirit that "they met hardship with joy and ardor and perhaps even sought it intentionally." Msgr. Sibillia would have liked the Assumptionists to increase as much as possible in the cities and in the civilized countryside of Chile, but it did not seem to Genocchi that this should prevent their being used in some missions because the more difficult the mission, the more it suited them.[15]

---

[15] *Ibid.*

CHAPTER III

THE SITUATION IN PERU

On September 12 Genocchi arrived in Lima and was greeted by Msgr. Quattrocchi. Because Msgr. Quattrocchi lived alone in the Apostolic Delegation he invited Genocchi to stay with him. Genocchi did this for almost the whole month he was to spend in Lima. "We get along together," Genocchi informed Cardinal Merry del Val, "to my great advantage."[1]

The first notes taken by Genocchi in Lima reveal him as conscientiously devoting himself to the study of laws and official decrees. He did this in order to support the demands that he made on public authorities. From *Colección de leyes, decretos, resoluciones, y otros documentos oficiales, referentes al Departamento de Loreto* Genocchi recorded the following information. It is central to an understanding of his mission.

In 1888 the "Obra de la Propagación de la Fé en el Oriente del Peru" was established.

May 1, 1894. Leo XIII wrote to the Peruvian bishops that they should increase the number of the missions among the Indians.

November 9, 1897. Iguitos was declared the capital of Loreto by the Peruvian Congress and President Nicolás de Pierola.

January 5, 1899. The Peruvian Congress passed a law which was promulgated on that date by the President, Don Nicolás de Pierola, granting an annual subvention of 3,000 soles [300 pounds] to be divided equally among the three Apostolic Prefectures. These had been established by a Presidential decree of October 27, 1898, with the assent and approbation of the Holy See, and were to be as follows:

(1) the Northern Prefecture, San León de Amazonas, to be coextensive with the national territories to the North of the rivers Maranon and Amazon. These were to separate it from;

(2) the Central Prefecture, or San Francisco de Ucayali, which was to comprise the original missions of the Franciscans of Ocopa, and from

---

[1] G. Genocchi to Cardinal R. Merry del Val, September 17, 1911. ASV.SS. F.4. 56-57. Msgr. David Quattrocchi was Chargé d'Affairs. The Apostolic Delegate to Peru was Msgr. Angelo Scapardini, 1910-1917.

(3) the Southern Prefecture, Santo Domingo de Urubamba, extending from the Urubamba River and its tributaries to the whole of the national territory to the East and South, and reaching up to the frontiers of Brazil and Bolivia.

The headquarters of these Prefectures were to be Iquitos, Ocopa, and Cuzco respectively, and it was arranged that they should be placed under the charge of the Augustinians, Franciscans, and Dominicans. In the decree of October 27, 1898, referred to above, paragraph G states: "The government will cede in the town of Iquitos a plot of land for the establishment of the headquarters of the Northern Prefecture, and will grant, according to the laws of the country and by means of the local authorities, effective protection to the Apostolic Prefectures and Missions."

May 3, 1899. Amendment of the general decree of October 27, 1898, concerning the building of the three Prefectures and 3,000 soles to be given to the said Prefectures.

January 22, 1900. Decree of the Sacred Congregation for the Propagation of the Faith concerning the establishment of the three Prefectures.

April 16, 1900. Official letter of the Apostolic Delegate Msgr. Pietro Gasparri.[2]

Genocchi judged it particularly important for his mission to record word for word two decrees concerning the facilities promised by the Peruvian government to the Prefect Apostolic of Iquitos:

Lima, July 4, 1903.

Since it is necessary to protect by all possible means the civilizing influence carried on by the Prefecture Apostolic of San León de Amazonas, we decree that the monthly allotted 25 pounds sterling (article 4415 of general budget) to the priests of Chasuta, Santa Catalina, Uchisa, Pachica, Balzapuerto, Jeveros, Lagunas, Andoas, Nauta, and Pebas, located in the jurisdiction of the above mentioned Prefecture, be handed every month by the Treasury of Iquitos to the Father Prefect of San Leon de Amazonas to use for carrying out his mission. He is ordered to give an annual report to the Minister of Justice.

(signed)
Orihuela

---

[2] AGG. S. 7/17. See Carlos Larrabure y Correa, *Colección de leyes, decretos, resoluciones, y otros documentos oficiales referentes al Departamento de Loreto* (Lima: Edición oficial, 1905), Vol. I, p. 217-219.

Lima, July 4, 1904.

Besides the sum indicated in article 4479 of the general budget, starting from this date and every month the Treasury of Iquitos will pay the sum of five pounds sterling for the said land that the government must grant to the Prefect Apostolic. This money is for the construction of an operating center.

(signed)
Eguiguren[3]

Genocchi was introduced by Msgr. Quattrocchi to the members of the Society called "Obra de la Propagación de la Fé en el Oriente del Peru". This society was composed of ladies from the principal families of Lima. It was founded in 1888 by Father Francisco de Sales Soto with the approval of the Archbishop of Lima. The purpose of the society was to revive the missions in the interior of Peru. These were at a low ebb after the Spanish war (1866-1871), the succeeding internal revolutions, the war with Chile (1879-1883), and the financial bankruptcy and ruin which followed the civil wars. This society published a small periodical entitled *Anales de la Obra de la Propagación de la Fé en el Oriente del Peru*. This periodical became an indispensable source of information for Genocchi. In 1900 the bulletin published the following item:

A REMARK

It is high time that the government should make its moderating action felt on the shores of the Amazon, Maranon, and other rivers. There are traders without conscience who carry cruelty to the point of carrying off wives and children from the homes of the unhappy savages. They enslave them after taking advantage of their unpaid services and corrupting their morals. One can understand that such procedure discredits the civilized life and the religion which nominally these soulless beings profess, thus driving the natives from the centers of population, and exposing honorable explorers, the missionaries, and even the authorities themselves, to the vengeance of the Indians. We do not believe the adoption of some system of vigilance and punishment to be so difficult. This would put an end to these enemies of their country and of humanity. It behooves the government delegate at Iquitos to propose something definite in the above sense. Otherwise, all that may be done for the colonization of the jungle Indians will be done in vain, owing to demoralization of the native tribes.[4]

---

[3] AGG. S. 7/17. See *Anales de la Obra de la Propagación de la Fé en el Oriente del Peru* (Hereafter *Anales*), October 1903, p. 111.

[4] *Anales*, Vol. II, p. 41.

As a result of this Remark, the Peruvian government established a Custom House under Francisco Zapatero, and a military post under Major Juan M. Gonzales, on the Putumayo River, in November of the same year.

In September 1901, Idelfonso Fonseca was appointed Peruvian *Comisario Fluvial* of the Putumayo River. About that time Colonel Pedro Portillo, a man who was familiar with the conditions of slavery existing in the jungle, was appointed Prefect of Loreto. He was charged with implementing various plans of improvement in this territory. During the following year, 1902, Colonel Portillo was aboard the Peruvian government launch, *Cahuapana*, traveling on the rivers Putumayo and Napo. He appointed a commission composed of Captain Enrique Espinar, Lieutenant Numa P. León, of the Peruvian navy, and a civil engineer, Garcia Rosel, to make maps and surveys of the Putumayo. At this time *Señor* Julio C. Arana was organizing the rubber exploitation of the Putumayo with the active official assistance of Prefect Portillo. Colonel Portillo was aware of the slave raids made by the Arana Company. Proof of that fact is the report made to the Prefect of Loreto by George M. von Hassel, a civil engineer in the employment of the Peruvian government, dated December 12, 1902, at Iquitos:

> The native tribes inhabiting the regions recently traversed by me are the following: the Amahuas and Remos on the Tamaya and upper Yurua rivers; the Piros, Marcos, Huarayos, Chontas, and Campas on the Manu; the Amahuaca and Inamalis on the Purus. I beg protection which you can afford, who are aware of the condition of these tribes from your explorations and your having lived in close contact with them, condemned as they are to disappear in a certain time. These tribes are the object of continual slave raids, undertaken in the majority of cases by whites who by these means enjoy a lucrative trade in human flesh. There are individuals who in a space of three or four years have sold over 390 of these poor beings. On account of bad treatment and sudden change in mode of life sixty per cent of the Indians caught in the slave raids die, not to take count of those killed in the course of the same.[5]

* * *

In December of 1900, Father Paulino Diaz, an Augustinian friar and native of Oviedo in Spain, arrived in Peru to take charge of the Prefecture Apostolic of San León de Amazonas. He was accompanied

---

[5] Peruvian Foreign Office: Archivio de limites. XX Century, title N. 1. Minute paper N. 5.

A *Comissario* was a quasi military officer with the function of a magistrate.

by Fathers Pedro Prat, Bernardo Calle and Placido Malo, along with a lay brother, Gonzalo Fernandez. These, like their superior, were all Spaniards. Father Diaz had some complaints to make in his report of January of 1902 to the President of the "Obra de la Propagación de la Fé en el Oriente del Peru." He said that his mail did not reach him, and that the local authorities were not carrying out the instructions of the government at Lima with respect to the land which was to be given to the Mission at Iquitos for a church and residence. He also stated that these authorities, far from offering him any assistance, seemed to put every possible obstacle in his way. At this point Colonel Portillo introduced Father Diaz to *Señor* Amadeo Burga. With this man's assistance, and under the direction of Father Calle, a mission was established at a place called Nazareth on the Maranon. Early in 1902 Colonel Portillo was anxious that a mission be established by Father Diaz on the Aquarico River, or Upper Napo. These territories were the scene of some conflicts with Ecuadorean troops; at Angosteros on July 26, 1903, and at Torres-Causana in July, 1904. These conflicts led both Ecuador and Peru to withdraw their forces from Napo to Quito and Iquitos, respectively.

In 1902, while Colonel Portillo proceeded to the Putumayo and Napo, he commissioned a certain Don Manuel Pablo Villanueva to travel on the Yura River, and organize there a system of improvement conceived by the Peruvian government. Already in 1894 the sources of this river and the Purus had been the scene of the "civilizing" activity of Peruvian rubber traders. Early in 1902 the local government of the Brazilian State of Amazonas decreed the establishment of a Brazilian Custom House post at the mouth of the Amonea River on the left bank of the Yura. This was brought about partly through the policy being developed at that time by the Bolivian government in the Acre territory, and partly by the work undertaken by Don Pablo Villanueva. As a result of this step the Prefect of Loreto dispatched an armed force, consisting of regular Peruvian troops and some Peruvian rubber traders under the Commissary Coudra to take possession of the sources of the Yura and Purus for Peru. In October, 1902, the armed force reached the confluence of the Yura with the Amonea and, on the eighteenth of that month, ambushed some Brazilians who were working on that side. This was one of the attacks which afterwards formed part of the subject matter of the Court of Arbitration between Brazil and Peru. These attacks continued from 1902 to 1904, as can be seen from the proceedings of this Peru-Brazilian Claim Court of Arbitration held in Rio de Janeiro. The minutes of this Court are a record of an outbreak of crime and slavery, very similar to those of the Putumayo.

In a letter dated June 2, 1902, Father Diaz wrote from Iquitos: "As for the missions which, at the suggestion of Prefect Portillo, were to be established on the Napo and Putumayo, the Prefect had just told me that for the present their establishment would not be possible, because of the disagreement existing in respect to frontiers between the Republics of Ecuador and Colombia." Father Diaz proposed, however, to reopen the old Jesuit mission of Peras where there was a large number of Indians, and from there he hoped to visit the Indians of the Igaraparana.[6]

In November 1903, the Peruvian government steamer *Putumayo* took to the Igaraparaná a large body of regular troops under the command of a *Señor* Albarracin. The *Anales de la Obra de la Propagación de la Fé en el Oriente del Peru* of 1903 published another letter of Father Diaz, dated December 6, 1903, in which he expressed his great desire to go to the Putumayo, which he called "the empire of Satan." In the same letter he complained that the authorities and the inhabitants of Iquitos opposed the mission in every possible way. A later volume of the *Anales de la Obra de la Propagación de la Fé en el Oriente del Peru* contained an undated but full report of the Apostolic Prefecture of San Leon de Amazonas:

> The majority of the national white race of Peruvians come from Cachapoyas and Mayobamba and from the regions of the coast, especially from those of the North, and here these latter are designated by the name of Limenos. Those of foreign white race are composed of nearly every nationality: Portuguese, Brazilians, Italians, Spaniards, Germans, French, English, Colombians, Ecuadorians, etc. There are also a good many Asiatics of yellow race.... Those of the pure native indigenous race without any crossbreeds, namely the Mayorunas and Pelas, who are the most numerous and are predominant on the lower Amazon, the Cocamas and Turapiscos on the lower Napo and on the upper Napo in the destroyed villages founded by the Jesuits on the Río Coca; on the central and upper Amazon, the Boyenos and Omaguas; on the lower Maranon, the Cocamas and Urasinas; and on the upper waters, the Jeveros and Cahuapanas tribes. On the Yavari River there are very few Peruvians, as most of the owners and peons there are Brazilians. What I have stated above is speaking generally, for, in consequence of the numerous and frequent sales and purchases of peons, justified under the name of transferring debts, more or less real, there is now a great mixture of these tribes as well as many others.
> Besides these Indians, known by the name of Cholos, there is another numerous contingent, generally devoted to domestic service. They are

---

[6] *Anales*, Vol. III, p. 295.

acquired by purchase or by inheritance or by other barbarous and criminal methods, from the many tribes of Indians which still dwell in distant forests, dragged by force from their homes, separated from their parents, brothers and relatives. Although as a rule well treated, they are nonetheless for all that, nothing other than true slaves in all the crudity of the word, without any hope of freedom from this bondage other than that of running away.

All the Indians mentioned so far are considered as civilized and as Christians, through their having been baptized, on some occasion by their owners parodying the ceremonies of the Church. As a matter of fact as regards religious or profane instruction, they hardly differ from the so-called heathen savages.[7]

In referring to the old mission, Father Diaz said that one's soul suffered "at the sight of so much desolation in the midst of that which cost so much sweat and fatigue to create: all destroyed in a short space of time by the greed of soulless men calling themselves 'the standard-bearers of civilization and progress.' " Nearly all the villages founded at one time on both shores of the Peruvian Amazon and Maranon Rivers were in the same or worse condition. Not so long ago, they were still flourishing but now they were completely destroyed. Their former inhabitants were dispersed among the rivers of Brazil or Bolivia, and were reduced to the most degrading and frightful slavery.[8]

On June 2, 1904, the Indians, driven to desperation by the caucheros, attacked the rubber station at Nazareth. Among those killed were Father Bernardo Calle and a secular priest named Muñoz. On October 13, 1905, Father Diaz wrote in the *Anales de la Obra de la Propagación de la Fé en el Oriente del Peru* that in the Pucu-curu there were many heathen Saparos Indians, but they were deep in the forests. They had been scared and driven there by the *caucheros* who had harried them to death. The same thing was taking place with the Indians of the Corrientes.

In May of 1907 Father Diaz went to Rome to report personally to the Holy See on the conditions prevalent in his district. He stated that on certain rivers of his Prefecture Apostolic it was "impossible to civilize the natives as long as the rubber traders continued their slave raids and other outrages which the pen hesitated to describe." [9] In November, 1908, having returned from Rome, he told of his desire to reach the Putumayo from the Napo River, and of the opposition with

---

[7] *Anales*, Vol. III, p. 201.
[8] *Anales*, Vol. III, p. 301.
[9] *Anales*, Vol. V, p. 388.

which his project was met. The missionary had lost heart as a result of
the antagonism and opposition with which his efforts had been
received. The priests at Iquitos found themselves in serious financial
problems owing to the suppression of the limited funding given to the
mission by the Peruvian government. The ladies of the Committee of
the "Obra de la Propagación de la Fé en el Oriente del Peru" petitioned
Congress of October 11, 1909, not to withhold the funding. They
stated:

> It is not here a question of distant colonies, neither of a simple sentiment
> of human dignity. It is on national soil that these offenses are committed
> (how often have the Prefects Apostolic asked for alms to ransom our
> Indians, and to prevent their being sold as slaves in Brazil?), and these
> unhappy Indians have no protection other than forty-one missionaries
> assisted and defended by a Society of Ladies.[10]

The Congress did not grant the petitioners' request.

* * *

In the same periodical of the "Obra de la Propagación de la Fé en
el Oriente del Peru," Genocchi found important information concerning the other two Prefectures Apostolic, San Francisco de Ucayali
and Santo Domingo de Urubamba. The January, 1911, issue of the
Anales de la Obra de la Propagación de la Fé en el Oriente del Peru featured a
report by Father Leandro Cornejo of the Prefecture of San Francisco de
Ucayali. He wrote, "Both to capture the savages for the first time, as
well as to regain possession of those who have escaped, a radical and
extreme method is employed which is called *correria* [slave raid]." Father
Cornejo described how slave raiding took place. The rubber traders,
united in groups of eight to ten and well-armed with Winchester
carbines, start off into the bush to hunt the Indians. The great skill of
the rubber traders in traversing the forest puts them in an advantageous
position to beat the Indians on their own ground. The soil, wet with
rain, is converted into a powerful ally for the rubber traders in their
slave raids because the tracks made by the footsteps of the Indians are
easily disclosed. When the rubber traders discover the camp, they
generally spend the whole night observing it. At daybreak, with loud
yells, lighted torches, and firing their rifles, they hurl themselves on the
unhappy Indians who, terrified, offer no resistence, endeavoring only to
escape.[11]

---

[10] *Anales*, Vol. VI, N. 3 January 1910.
[11] *Anales*, Vol. VI, p. 198.

In 1902 Father Ramon Zubieta of the Dominican Order reached Cuzco and took charge of the Southern Prefecture of Santo Domingo de Urubamba. This mission seems to be the one which met with least opposition on the part of the civil authorities. Nevertheless, the *Anales de la Obra de la Propagación de la Fé en el Oriente del Peru* recorded a letter dated November 10, 1905, written by the Dominican José Palacio from Paucartambo, a town only a few miles from Cuzco:

> You will already have been informed of the raid made by savages on the *Hacienda Asunción*, and how they were driven back with great loss by the forces of the Commissary stationed in that valley. The news reached this town at once by telephone, and caused much alarm to all the inhabitants. The ferocious Chunchos Huachipaires surprised the forces of this Commissary, and those who were not killed in the fight remain prisoners in the hands of our brave police.
>
> This is what was at first stated, but I was surprised that in an attack previously prepared by the Chunchos, they should have been completely routed without having hit a single one of their enemies. And in fact the true state of the case appears to be a very different matter. Here is substantially what took place, the relation of which one cannot hear with indifference.
>
> Seven unhappy Campas Indians, two of whom were women, accustomed to frequenting the peons of the state who were themselves employed to work in the jungle, committed the dreadful sin of taking four *yuccas* from one of the fields of the estate (when thousands of times the employees of the same had destroyed theirs). Fearing no one, as they had not injured any person, they were quietly eating the roots near the fire which they had lighted to roast them. The smoke betrayed the place where they were. Our brave police, coming upon them suddenly from the *Caserío* [house of the workers on an estate or *hacienda*], surrounded them on all sides without any warning and without telling them of their crime. Then they concentrated their rifle fire on these unhappy beings, leaving four dead bathed in their blood and taking prisoner the others, who offered no resistance. I have just spoken at this moment with the three survivors, sent here as prisoners of war, and it breaks my heart to hear from their lips of so much wickedness.
>
> This took place in the absence of the worthy head of the police station, my excellent friend Solar, who would have prevented such a lamentable event from taking place.[12]

* * *

From all this documentation Genocchi drew the following conclusions. Slave raids were of common occurrence throughout the

---

[12] *Anales*, Vol. IV, p. 188.

Peruvian jungle. Up to that time, the authorities had done nothing to
end the practice. On some occasions the Peruvian government officials
had even assisted the *caucheros* in their raids. It was true that the conduct
of the Peruvian government officials was in part due to the political and
military dispute about the boundaries of Peru, Brazil and Colombia.
This political situation was also a reason for the difficulty in establishing missions among the Indians. In addition Father Diaz and his
confreres were Spaniards and, as foreigners, were not well accepted by
the Peruvians.

At the conclusion of Genocchi's meetings with the committee of
the "Obra de la Propagación de la Fé en el Oriente del Peru," it was
decided, in accordance with the recommendation of Msgr. Quattrocchi,
to promote a subscription of money for the needs of a mission to be
established among the Indians. And so it was that, on February 9, 1912,
Genocchi sent Cardinal Merry del Val a packet with several lists of
subscriptions in homage to the Holy Father. This money was raised by
the ladies of Lima. In Iquitos they were able to collect about 300
signatures and 145 Italian lire.[13]

---

[13] G. Genocchi to Cardinal R. Merry del Val, 9 February 1912. ASV.SS. F.4. 88.

CHAPTER IV

ENGANCHE OR SERVITUDE FOR DEBT

At Lima the Pontifical Visitor found a strong supporter of his work in the Consul General of England, Mr. Lucien Jerome. Genocchi informed Cardinal Merry del Val that the British representative could not have been more obliging and courteous. Jerome was advised of Genocchi's arrival by his government which urged him to help Genocchi as much as he could; he did not fail to do so. Jerome, who was a fervent Catholic, had put so much energy into anti-slavery propaganda in Peru that he made himself rather troublesome to his government. In November the newly appointed Consul General would come to Lima and Jerome would go on to London, where he intended to remain with his family. There, near the central government, he would be able to continue the work he had begun with so much zeal. Genocchi remarked, "No one is better prepared for it than he." [1]

---

[1] G. Genocchi to Cardinal R. Merry del Val, October 7, 1911. ASV.SS. F.4.75. On July 25, 1911, Lucien Jerome had transmitted to Msgr. D. Quattrocchi the following exchange of telegrams between the British Legation in Lima and the Foreign Office. For the use of the Apostolic Delegation the telegrams were translated into Italian by G. Genocchi upon his arrival in Lima.

"1. London, July 21st, 1911.

His Majesty's Government considers that a religious mission should be established in the Putumayo with Headquarters at Iquitos whereby considerable good would be derived. Peruvian Government should give positive proof of their good intentions by not only giving missionaries every facility but should grant them a substantial annual subsidy. GREY.

2. Lima, July 22nd.

Owing to provisions of Peruvian Constitution we would be precluded making suggestion for establishing Protestant Mission. I am, however, in a position to report that action is now being taken by the Archbishop of Lima and the Papal delegate. Tomorrow meeting attended by ladies and others of high social standing. My endeavours are now directed to secure strong current public opinion. JEROME.

3. London, July 24th.

Difficulty with regard to Protestant Mission appreciated. Glad to learn Archbishop of Lima is taking the matter up in cooperation with papal delegate. It will therefore not be necessary for you to suggest Protestant Mission to President, but you must inform me as to readiness of Peru to encourage and support efforts of clergy. GREY, ASV.DP. F.4.654.

During the first two weeks Genocchi met twice with the English representative. Genocchi informed him that, from what he had seen and learned in Peru, he had reached the conclusion that the conditions of the Indians in the Amazon were much worse than those of the Negroes in the Congo. According to the instructions received from the Secretary of State he was required to visit Bolivia, but now the Vatican was directing him to proceed to Iquitos with the least possible delay. He had decided, consequently, to set out for Iquitos about the middle of October. At that time he was informed by Jerome that Casement had decided to go to the Putumayo a second time and that he had left Southampton on August 16.

After his inquiry in the Putumayo, Casement returned to London at the end of 1910. While working on the completion of his detailed report, he wrote to Sir Edward Grey that it was a matter of great urgency to deal with the list which he had compiled of some of the worst criminals of the Putumayo. All of them were charged with the most atrocious crimes against the Indians. In particular he insisted on the need for immediate action, as the criminals were almost in debt to the Company and, consequently, had no reason for delaying their escape, should they fear legal action. Nevertheless, after the return of Casement and the commission, three full months were to pass before the complete report of Casement's investigation would be given to the Foreign Office. It was not until April of 1911 that the British government sent its first instruction to the British Minister in Peru. He had to inform the Peruvian government confidentially about the crimes committed against the Indians, and to invite the government to take steps to punish the criminals as well as to prevent a recurrence of the atrocities. Casement was waiting with growing impatience for the announcement of some real action against the perpetrators of the crimes. At the end of April the first reply came from Peru, stating that Judge Paredes had set out on a gunboat and would spend three months investigating the situation. In the meantime, many of the accused had escaped. Questions were brought up in the British Parliament which compelled the Foreign Office to press for more satisfactory answers from Peru. In the beginning of July the Foreign Office put more pressure on Peru to give tangible proof that it was determined to eradicate the existing abuses in the Putumayo. Casement, disconcerted by the delay, asked in August to return to the Putumayo to undertake a second personal investigation in order to ascertain what steps, if any, were actually being taken.

In the course of their meeting in the middle of September, Genocchi told Jerome that he was "very anxious to get in touch with

Casement."[2] By that time, however, Casement was already in Manaus. From there he was to leave for Iquitos, where he would arrive on October 16. Genocchi did not reach Iquitos until December 23. On December 7, Casement had already boarded the *Ucayali* for Belém do Pará on his way back to England. It was probably at this meeting of Genocchi with Jerome that the English representative gave him Casement's reports addressed to Sir Edward Grey and dated March 17 and 21, 1911.

* * *

The second report relates the depositions of thirty natives of Barbados, victims themselves and — a fact to make one shudder with horror — compulsory agents in inflicting tortures on the Indians. They were English subjects residing in Iquitos, La Chorrera, Matanzas, and Ultimo Retiro. Casement questioned them from September through December in 1910. Genocchi, in the interest of his mission, recorded portions of those statements in his notes. There are four pages full of atrocities so shocking that they defy detailed description.

Frederick Bishop testified that Joshua Dyall, one of the natives of Barbados, was accused of having had relations with an Indian woman belonging to a white man and was placed on the stocks. The holes were small, so Dyall's leg started bleeding when the chief of Ultimo Retiro pressed down on the stocks with the weight of his body. After a few hours the stocks was turned over and Dyall revolved at full speed all night. The following morning a chain was placed around his neck and he was hauled up so that his feet barely touched the ground.

Several peons had between twenty and thirty wives. A certain Martingui, upon discovering that one of his Indian girls was infected with syphilis, tied her up high, flogged her and had her branded in the genital area. Bishop related that flogging was done in many ways. One way, practiced at all stations, was to run a chain which gripped the victim's neck along a V-shaped post. The chain was pulled taut and the victims then whipped. Death often resulted.

Adolphus Gibbs told of an Indian who had been in the stocks but managed to slip out of the chain and escape because he had become very thin. Augusto Jimenez sent a young man of about eighteen after him. The Indian was soon found and brought back. Jimenez then ordered the boy to chop off the Indian's head. The same fate befell a Boras Indian.

---

[2] L. Jerome to E. Grey, September 26, 1911. PRO.FO. 42933.

Stanley Lewis witnessed an Indian chief who was left for a long time in the stocks in the black hole because his people had fled the rubber plantation. The black hole was a cellar built under the house. José Innocent Fonseca ordered Lewis to kill the chief. Lewis refused, and he himself was then put in the stocks for two days without food. Genocchi quoted *verbatim*:

> I have seen Indians killed for sport, tied up to trees and shot at by Fonseca and others. After they had been drinking they would sometimes do this. They would take a man out of the stocks, tie him to a tree and shoot, using him as a target. I have often seen the Indians killed thus, and also shot after they had been flogged and their flesh had become rotten with maggots. Others I have seen killed by the Indian boys being trained as *muchachos*.[3] These boys were armed with *machetes*, and they would cut off the victim's head against the tree-stumps. I once saw Fonseca himself killing one of his young girls because she allowed a child of his, whom she was carrying, to put a leaf of tobacco in its mouth.

Genocchi recorded from Casement's long interrogation with James Chase that in May, 1910, Jermin Vasquez, two other Peruvians and eight *muchachos* were sent by Abelardo Aguero to look for runaway Indians. A Boras Indian named Katenere had escaped with a band of his fellow Indians. They took some rifles with them and shot Bartoleme Zumaeta, the brother-in-law of Julio C. Arana. The group searching for the Indians, led by Vasquez, made a few stops along the way. In the first Indian house they reached, the members of the expedition caught five men and three women. At the next house they caught four Indians, one woman and three men. Vasquez, simply because he was in command and could do whatever he liked, ordered one of the *muchachos* to cut the woman's head off. The *muchacho* held her by grabbing her hair, then he flung her down and with more than one blow of the *machete* severed her head. Continuing their search, the group captured some other Indians, among whom was Katenere's wife. Katenere later came to see his wife, as Vasquez had anticipated. Katenere killed a *muchacho*, but that evening he himself was killed. On the following morning the search was resumed. Along the way they came upon a child, a little girl of about six or eight years of age. Terrified at the sight of the armed men and of the Indians bound in chains, she began to cry. Vasquez at once ordered a very young *muchacho* named Cherey, a Recigiro Indian boy, to cut her head

---

[3] *Muchacho* (English - boy) is used in R. Casement's report to designate a young Indian taken from one tribe and trained to terrorize in another district people who were not his immediate kinsmen. The *machete* was a hunting knife.

off. According to Katenere's wife, this child, murdered solely because she was crying, was Katenere's daughter by another wife. The same fate, immediate decapitation by Cherey, befell a woman prisoner and an Indian boy of about fifteen or sixteen, simply because they could not keep up with the group. Three Indian men, weak from hunger and not able to keep up were shot, one by Vasquez, the other two by Cherey. When they finally arrived at Morella, only five prisoners were alive; one woman, three men, and a child. Immediately one man was suspended in the usual way with his toes touching the ground. The others were placed in the stocks, except for the child who was untied and placed near his mother. The following morning they went on foot and without water to the station of Abissinia, a five- to seven-hour walk.

Stanley Sealy gave the following account: Jimenez went with the *muchachos* on the search for fugitives. He found an old woman, but she was not able to tell him anything. He led her to the camp. The next morning he ordered a *muchacho* to hang her with her arms tied behind her back and to gather dry leaves and burn them under her feet. He then had her untied and told an Indian: "If she is not able to walk, cut her head off." The Indian did so. Later he met two women, one with a child. Jimenez asked the latter: "Where are the Indians who have run away?" She did not know. Jimenez ordered the Indian leader of the muchachos to cut off the child's head. The mother screamed, and she was tied up with the other woman. They then found a strong and robust Indian and took him captive. Jimenez asked him: "Where is there a rowboat to cross the Caquetá?" The Indian answered, "I do not know." He was bound with his hands behind his back and hanged from a tree. Jimenez struck a match and lit the dry leaves under his feet. The Indian began to burn. After a long slow torture he was shot. Another witness, John Brown, testified that in Morelia, Jimenez killed twelve Indians who had been taken prisoners because they had escaped and were of no use to him.

Genocchi recorded this statement of Joshua Dyall:

> Normand made me kill an Indian who was in chains so that he could take his wife. Normand held the slave's legs apart, and ordered me to crush his genitals with a club. I obeyed and we killed him. We killed another in the same way because he had escaped. Another was killed by beating because he had tried to escape.

Genocchi wrote down the testimony of two eyewitnesses, Westerman Leavine and Clifford Quintin, concerning the same man, Armando Normand. Leavine stated that in 1907 Normand killed three old Indians and their two young daughters in cold blood. Their bodies were devoured by dogs. Ordinarily he left the Indians in the stocks to die of starvation and gangrene. He burned an Indian chief alive in the presence of his wife and two children. Then he beheaded the wife, dismembered the children, and threw all of them into the fire. He cut to pieces an Indian woman because she did not want to prostitute herself to an employee. He wrapped another woman in a Peruvian flag, drenched her with kerosene and then set her on fire in order to make her reveal where her parents were hidden. Many men and women, their hands tied behind their backs, were thrown alive into a fire prepared by the *muchachos*. Three male natives were tied together in a row. Then, using his mauser rifle, Normand shot all of them with one bullet. Quintin stated that, in one case, Normand caught all the Indians of a large family, women, men, and young children, some barely a month old. All were killed. Normand himself decapitated them all, except the little children. These were abandoned in the house to die of starvation. He did this because the Andokes had killed some white people. Another time the *muchachos* brought an Indian chief named Nequen to Normand. Normand himself then poured kerosene over the Indian's head, lit the man's hair and threw him on the fire where he burned alive. A captured Indian chief refused to reveal to Normand the whereabouts of his people. Both his hands and feet were cut off and he was left to die on the forest trail.

The last instance cited by Genocchi was that of the brutality of a man named Abelardo Aguero who killed purely for sport, according to a witness named James Mapp. One person was done away with because he had only one foot and was not able to walk. In 1906, on his return from Iquitos where he had gone for a health treatment, Aguero found about eight recently-captured Indians in the stocks. He had a few drinks and then ordered them to be killed. Four other Indians had been hung up by their arms, which were twisted behind their backs, and had been kept this way for about three or four hours. After that, swinging them playfully, Hilary Quales, a 24-year-old man, began to bite them tearing off pieces of flesh. One of the victims, angered when bitten in the legs and thighs, kicked Quales, who retaliated by biting off and spitting away the man's little toe. Throughout Aguero was looking on and laughing. Subsequently the four, all young men, were put back in the stocks.[4]

* * *

---

[4] AGG. S. 7/12.

During their second meeting the Apostolic Visitor and the representative of the British government dealt with the need for legislation in favor of the Indians. L. Jerome related to the Foreign Office that Father Genocchi was particularly "impressed with the urgent necessity of legislation" to protect the unfortunate natives of the inland forest. Msgr. Quattrocchi had already secured in this view the cooperation of an influential group of members of the Chambers of Deputies. At Genocchi's request Jerome gave him a copy of the Memorandum about *Enganche* or Servitude for Debt in Peru which Jerome had sent to the Foreign Office.[5] In it the English Chargé d'Affaires pointed out that the existing law of Peru made quasi-slavery, or peonage, not only possible but perfectly legal.

Before addressing the question of the law, the Memorandum examined the attitude of the country toward this aspect of the labor problem. During the year 1910, the Lima "Sociedad Pro- Indigena" had been engaged in a very active campaign on behalf of the native races to check abuses arising out of the system of peonage known in Peru as *Enganche*. Conducted perhaps without sufficient prudence, accusations were made that the leaders of the association had used the campaign as a cloak for blackmail. Earlier a serious charge of real slavery had been brought by the "Sociedad Pro-Indigena" against a certain *Señor* Alvarino, a landowner in the valley of Chachamayo. He replied to the allegation with a counter-charge of slander against *Señor* Guylen, the honorary secretary of the "Sociedad Pro-Indigena."

On September 21, 1911, the semi-official paper of Lima, *El Diario*, used the occasion of Alvarino's petition against the "Sociedad Pro-Indigena" to express the views of the ruling class in the matter of labor problems. Without accepting the terms in which the petition was drawn up, the newspaper stated that the mode of procedure adopted by the "Sociedad Pro-Indigena" in the fulfillment of its task was alienating it from the object for which the association was organized.

> The regeneration of the Indians is a complex problem. It demands not only altruism but, above all, the cooperation of scientists, of politicians, who do not allow themselves to be carried away by the brilliance of ideals. Along with rights which belong to the Indian as an individual, as a factor in industry, as a member of the body politic, we have to consider inveterate customs, habits existing for centuries which cannot be broken from one day to another, for then the cure would be worse than the disease. A gradual evolution must be sought such as the intelligent physician seeks to obtain in strengthening the worn organism of an invalid.

---

[5] L. Jerome to E. Grey, September 26, 1911. PRO.FO. 43940.

According to the newspaper, "to sustain to the utmost every complaint that is brought up by the natives, spontaneously or maliciously, and to give them publicity without an investigation that would prove the truth of the statement made," was hardly the best method to realize those counsels of sane reason. By these proceedings, rather than obtaining a proper defense of the Indians, "we are in danger of running into a class war and a fearful disagreement between the working-class and the capitalists whose interests, in fact do not clash." One requires the other to subsist in order to contribute to individual comfort and the progress of the country.

Because the newspaper judged the subject of great national importance, it published the following statement about the association in *La Patria* of Huancayo in February of the same year:

PRO-INDIGENA

A few months ago an association was founded in Lima with the noble object indicated by the words heading these lines. In many cases the native race of Peru has been, and is, exploited by speculators devoid of all humanity. In many other cases, however, the native substitutes intelligence and education with habitual malice and turns to lies and slander as a means of retaliation on the employer who obliges him to work and does not permit him to elude his engagements. We propose to deal with two points which are today treated with great zeal by the "Sociedad Pro-Indigena".

This first is the *Contrato de Enganche* which is sanctioned by the authorities and to which the association is trying to put an end. Without any doubt in principle the idea of subjecting an individual to a kind of temporary slavery, which *Enganche* implies, is repugnant to altruistic minds.

Nevertheless, if these same gentlemen had practical occasion to appreciate the necessity of such a system, they would recognize that, in the actual condition of the development of the inhabitants of the Sierra, there is no other manner of obtaining labor. The suppression of the *Enganche* will bring with it serious consequences both to mining and agricultural industries.

The Indian only seeks work when pressed by his creditors or when filled with the desire to seek money for his festivals. Naturally he begins by asking for a large advance and as soon as he is able to dispose of the money received, he tries to evade the contract by escaping either to the mountains or to the coast. To prevent this, the patron must secure the *enganchado* by means of a deed or document with a surety and even a lien [hypothecation] or mortgage should the workman have any estate. Without such formality the employer or the *enganchador* would certainly lose his money. In the Andine centers of population, every form of work, even that connected with domestic servants, requires an *escritura* [written agreement]. Without this requisite the servant would abandon his work on the first opportunity.

The other point relates to public works or to communal labor for general benefit. In this respect it is necessary to bear in mind that in the matter of taxation the Indian is a privileged being. He pays hardly any taxes such as those contributed by the citizens of most civilized states. He does not worry about customs duties, for he hardly makes use of any imported article. Rustic and urban rates are not levied on his estate which he holds in common. In fact he contributes to support the charges of the State only through his share in the alcohol tax.

It is therefore very right and natural that he should contribute with his brawn to works of public benefit, to which the other citizens contribute with their money in the form of direct and indirect taxation. On the day when the privileges that the communities now enjoy disappear, and the land, divided up among the members of the communities, is subjected to the general system of taxation, the Indian will acquire the right of not being subjected to a tax in personal labor, which today is only a just compensation.

There was no doubt that *El Diario* reflected the views of the majority of the employers of labor. In their anxiety to secure labor, they quite overlooked the ethical side of the question. The Memorandum reported a recent decision on the part of the Supreme Court of Peru concerning the legality of the *Enganche* contract. These contracts were compared to the articles of agreement made between a captain of a merchant vessel and his crew. This removed any doubt as to the legality of the contract. Jerome noted that this system was not confined to Peru, but he believed that Peru was one of the Spanish-American states in which it was not only a question of custom but also of actually having the sanction of law.

Since the separation of the various Spanish-American countries from the Spanish Crown, nearly all the new republics had more or less adopted imitations of the French system of the codification of the laws introduced under the supervision of Cambaceres. The codes differed widely from those of the French and also from each other. In some instances the codes were adaptations from the *Recopilación de Leyes de Indias* of the Spanish Crown. Sometimes the codes were taken bodily from those of another country, i.e., the Civil Code of the Republics of Ecuador and Colombia. In Bolivia, Spanish usage and Spanish law of the colonial period continued to prevail. As a rule, Spanish laws relating to land titles had been adhered to in the majority of the republics. According to these laws the lands carried with them *droits des seigneurs* over the serfs or Indians dwelling on the estates. *De facto* in Peru, and *de jure* in Bolivia, those rights could be transferred by purchase from one owner to another, just as cattle on an estate could be transferred by deed in a European country. The laws relating to procedure in civil and criminal trials in South American republics were entirely different from the practices in British, French or American Courts of Law. The same could be said of the conveyancing and auxiliary departments of the courts of Justice. Courts of Equity were not recognized; nor was equity part of jurisdiction.

In a second part, the Memorandum treated the question of the legislation. Servitute for Debt had been prohibited by law in the British Empire and in the United States. The English Act uses the word pawn to indicate a person in such servitude. The American Federal Statute of March 2, 1867, uses the word peon.[6] The Peruvian civil code in the preliminary chapter, articles three and eight, established that:

> No one can be prevented from taking any action not prohibited by law. The Justices cannot set aside the application of the law, neither may they come to a verdict except by what is indicated in the same.

In the third book concerning "Obligations and Contracts," section two, chapter three, the civil code included the following articles:

> 1632. A person may engage him- (or her-)self to lend his (or her) services to another for domestic or industrial purpose for a certain time or for a certain enterprise.

> 1633. In regard to the settlement, payment or the rendering of accounts of day-laborers or wages of domestics the word of their lord receives entire faith unless the contrary can be proven.

> 1635. Servants may leave (their situation) when they please, **unless they have received advances in money or payment. In which case having received the same, they will be obliged to serve for the time and price agreed upon** [Jerome's emphasis], unless cause for their departure be shown.

Concerning the "Regulations as to Rural Police," the decree of January 1, 1878, stated the following articles in chapter one:

> 6. It is the duty of the rural commissaries:

> B. Not to permit loafing in fields or road by unknown unemployed persons.

---

[6] The word peon, pawn (Old English - pawnee) from Old French *pan*, and the German *pfant* (Old German - *pfand*), means gage or pledge. Spanish *peón* means a foot-soldier or pawn, but most commonly *peón* means a day-laborer who in Spanish America, at the time of Genocchi's inquiry, was like a serf, compelled to work for his creditor until his debts are paid.

Huitoto Indians and Barbados negro overseer

P. Not to allow the peons, be they contracted or day laborers, to be out of the estate to which they belong during working hours unless they have a written certificate from their master stating the reason for their permission to be away from the estate.

S. To take scrupulous care that the contracted laborers fulfill punctually the terms of their agreement on the estates to which they belong and that the masters be exact in rewarding them with the price of their labor in accordance with what had been stipulated. Any complaints arising from one or other cause will be settled by the terms of the contract.

T. Not to permit the *hacendados* [landowners] to sequester or hide laborers contracted on other estates and to impose on transgressors the fine or arrest which the gravity of the offense may require.

25. Any person who dedicates himself to the work of the field, either as day laborer or as servant of any kind, must carry an identification showing that he is so employed. ...

26. Herdsmen, woodgatherers, weeders, and their peons shall carry a similar identification which will be furnished them by the *hacendado* on whose estate they are.
(N.B. The above may be men who live in town and whose work may by chance carry them to the country, such as herdsmen employed by butchers, etc. [Jerome's remark]).

27. Servants and domestics, day laborers and other persons referred to in the two preceding articles, must secure from their respective masters, in order to leave their service, a written certificate vouching for their conduct and character. In case of refusal (by master) without just cause, they may apply to the commissary.

28. *Hacendados* may refuse to grant a character reference only in the event of the workman (or woman) **being indebted** [Jerome's emphasis] to the estate; but cannot refuse it in the event of bad conduct on the part of the person employed, in which case he must state this in the character reference.

The above decree was signed in Lima on December 11, 1877, but there is no doubt that its stipulation was still in effect in 1911. In September, 1911, the butler of the British Legation was kept in prison for a whole day because he left his *boleto* [identification] at home, notwithstanding his insistence on being employed at a Legation. His plight was discovered by chance and the man was released, but the authority made no apology. This example clearly demonstrates the state of the law in Peru respecting labor, and, hence, the importance of securing legislation making slavery illegal.

The Memorandum contained additional information concerning legislation in Ecuador, Colombia and Bolivia, information which was invaluable to Genocchi. Ecuador had many constitutions. The most recent, that of 1897, provided:

> Art. 21. There are not, neither will there be, slaves in the Republic, and anyone putting his foot on Ecuadorian soil, will become free.

> Art. 23. No one can be obliged to render services not imposed by law; and in no case can artisans or laborers be obliged to work unless it be in accord with the stipulation of a contract.

Similar articles were part of the constitution of Colombia, with almost the same words. The civil codes of the republics of Ecuador and Colombia had been taken in fact from the Chilean civil code. The articles of book IV, chapter 26, §7 of the Ecuadorian Civil Code, concerning "The Lease of Domestic Servants and Laborers," were identical to those of the civil code of Colombia:

> 1972. In the lease of domestic servants and laborers one of the contracting parties agrees to lend to the other certain services in exchange for a salary specified in the contract or according to the custom of the country.

> 1973. The service of domestics and laborers may be contracted for a determined time; but it cannot be stipulated to last more than one year, unless this stipulation is made in writing; and even with such a stipulation, the servant or the laborer cannot be obliged to remain for longer than five years to be counted from the date of the written agreement. Such an agreement may be indefinitely renewed. The time will be obligatory on both parties, unless otherwise agreed.

> 1974. Should no time be specified, it will cease at the good pleasure of either party. Besides, the servant or laborer cannot leave unexpectedly causing serious inconvenience and prejudice to the employer. He (or she) must remain in the position until he (or she) can be replaced even if no time as to notice may have been stipulated.

In Chile, Ecuador and Colombia the law provided that on the death of an employer his (or her) heirs or assignees would have to carry on the contract or pay a sum equivalent to the amount that would have been earned. Servants and laborers were not entitled to receive more than two month's wages in advance, and they could claim immediate payment for over one month's arrears.

Article 21 in the "Treaty of Friendship, Commerce and Navigation" between the republics of Colombia and Ecuador, signed at Quito August 10, 1905, stipulated: "The two contracting parties bind themselves to preserve the laws and regulations now in force in both republics respecting the abolition of the slave trade, and to take whatever measures may appear necessary in order to prevent the citizens or inhabitants of either of them from engaging themselves in having anything to do with such traffic."

The penal code and code of criminal procedure of the Republic of Ecuador showed that no particular regulations were in force under this heading. But information obtained from people who had resided in Colombia and Ecuador affirmed that in neither country did *Enganche* or peonage exist as it existed in Peru. In Chile, the native working man or *roto*, was quite able to care for himself and, indeed, he was much closer to the working man of Europe than was the worker of any other Ibero-American country (except Argentina).

The constitution of Bolivia stated in article three: "No slavery exists in Bolivia. Every slave as soon as he puts foot on Bolivian soil is free." However, a peculiar form of slavery known as *Pongaso* (and the slave as *pongo*) did exist. From the account of travellers it was known that slave conditions existed in the Department of La Paz itself, and in that of Yungas, Beni and the *Distrito de Colonias*. Bolivian troops were constantly employed in the suppression of native uprisings. It was believed that slave markets existed at Riberalta and on the Bolivian River Madre de Dios.

In 1839, Lord Henry J. T. Palmerston proposed the negotiation of a treaty with the Republic of Bolivia for the suppression of slave trade. In his letter to the English representative at Sucre he declared, "Her Majesty's Government hopes that Bolivia will not be the last state in the New World to concur with their fellow Christians in the Old [World] in putting an end to a system of crime, which has so long continued to disgrace the character of civilized nations." However, slave trade at that time was only considered in regard to African slavery which existed in Bolivia solely in the remote district of Santa Cruz de la Sierra. Lord Palmerston did not have in mind the state of affairs in regard to the condition of slavery to which the native races of America had been reduced by rubber traders or by mine owners and agriculturists. In conformity with the stipulation of the treaty of September 25, 1840, between Great Britain and Bolivia, José Ballivian promulgated a law declaring that slave trade carried on under the Bolivian flag was piracy. This law, however, specifically mentioned that it was made because of, and as part of, the treaty in question. This treaty had since been denounced by Bolivia. No new stipulations on the subject were entered upon between Great Britain and Bolivia in the Treaty of Commerce signed shortly before at La Paz. From a note written to the English representative at Chuquisaca by the Bolivian Minister of Foreign Affaires on September 19, 1844, it was clear that slavery was at that

time still a recognized institution in Bolivia. The note also spoke clearly
of the slaves as Negroes. The Indians were not mentioned.

The *Enganche* system was fully in use in the Republic of Bolivia.
Gangs of Indians from the plateau land were contracted for, more or
less under official pressure from corrupt authorities. They were then
compelled to work in the rubber lands of the Yungas, from which they
never returned. Bolivian laborers, especially from Cochabamba and its
surroundings, were also contracted to work in the *Nitrate Officinas* of
Chile. In this case the Bolivian authorities complained because the men
who went to Chile generally remained there.

The Memorandum concluded by quoting the opinion of the
American journalist, George W. Chrichfield, about the South American
labor problem. Jerome admitted that Chrichfield was too profuse in the
use of condemnatory adjectives, which weakened his arguments.
However, he had some good to say about the work of Chrichfield. "It
was one of the most scathing indictments ever penned against the
governments of Spanish America, well worth the perusal as a graphic
picture of the lack of morals, which made this section of the world what
it was at that time and explained how this state of affairs in the Amazon
region was possible and the magnitude of the difficulties which had to
be met to put a stop to it."[7]

* * *

In his letters Genocchi mentions his contacts with the officials of
the Peruvian government and the fact that the Minister of Cult gave
him letters of introduction to the Prefect of Iquitos. There are no details
of these diplomatic meetings, except a reference to the fact that, along
with Msgr. Quattrocchi, Genocchi manifested to the Peruvian
government the necessity of modifying the existing legislation, which
ratified a form of slavery. Along with an Italian translation of Jerome's
Memorandum written by Genocchi for the use of the Apostolic
Delegation, there is a draft of a proposal for the Peruvian Penal Code
concerning the crimes against freedom. Composed with the help of
Jerome, this draft probably represents the suggestion submitted to the
Peruvian government to prohibit even a disguised slavery, and slave
trade of the Indians.

> Section eleven of the Penal Code of Peru, regarding the crimes against
> freedom, etc., under the Title I, "Attempts against Freedom," contains
> the following Article 300:

---

[7] AGG. S.7/28. ASV.DP. F.4. 159-175.

"He who deprives another of his freedom by imprisoning or by detaining him, and he who provides a home or place for the detention or jailing, will be subject to substantial imprisonment:

1. if the deprivation of freedom lasts more than one month;
2. if it was done under pretense of public authority;
3. if there has been a death threat towards the one who has been deprived of freedom, or if anyone has committed any injury which does not deserve a higher punishment."

This article should be modified or enforced in the following manner, or following sense: "He who deprives another of his freedom to take advantage of his service or of his possessions, or by imprisoning him, etc. ...."

The following number should also be added:

4. "He who knowingly picks up a person of Indian race, and who takes advantage of his ignorance regarding his rights, in order to submit him to a condition of slavery and exploit his services deceitfully."

The proposal ended with this recommendation, **"In any case the punishment should be** the one which is mentioned in Article 32 of Title II of the Penal Code, that is to say, **the more severe penalty provided by said Article."** [Genocchi's emphasis] [8]

---

[8] AGG. S.7/28. See also Jerome's letter to Msgr. D. Quattrocchi, October 5, 1911. ASV.DP. F.4. 201.

CHAPTER V

THE ATROCITIES AGAINST THE INDIANS
AND THE SILENCE OF THE POPE

The Putumayo occurrences were brought to the public's attention by the American engineer, William E. Hardenburg. The London weekly *The Truth* was the first to disclose Hardenburg's statements concerning the atrocities committed against the Indians. The information was published in a series of articles dated from September to November of 1909. After some hesitancies due to the need of ascertaining evidence of the facts, the English press began to deal with this problem. At the same time questions were raised about responsibility for such crimes.

La Prensa of September 20, 1911, had translated an article entitled "The Crimes of the Putumayo" published in the August 10, 1911 issue of *The Daily News*. This gave Genocchi the opportunity to respond to the open or implied judgment and criticism of the English press against the Peruvian government and the Catholic Church. Genocchi's statement appeared as an editorial in the September 27, 1911 issue of the Lima daily *El Bien Social*. Genocchi praised the Peruvian press for dealing with "that disgusting subject." Because the European press (especially the English) had dealt with the crimes committed in Putumayo, it was necessary that the Peruvian press deal with them in order to form a public opinion which would lead to an efficacious remedy. Genocchi continued:

> The Peruvian government, in a most praiseworthy way, has begun to work energetically, sending a magistrate to the place, and imprisoning all those criminals upon whom hands can be laid. However, the honor of the country, compromised in the eyes of the world by a few evil men, will not be fully restored unless the whole country, in all social classes, unanimously protests openly against the barbarous iniquities perpetuated, and demands that they be in every possible way repressed and stopped. In order for this goal to be reached the local press must help, and *La Prensa* is to be praised because with the publication of yesterday's edition it began to give support.

The article of *The Daily News* narrated revolving facts in the simple language of two Indians who escaped the massacre and went to live in

London. However, Genocchi pointed out two inexact statements in the English newspaper. The first was: "The great criminal is Peru and Peru alone." The second, expressed in the form of a question: "Peru is a Catholic country: why didn't the head of the Church make a public protest against such barbarities?" Regarding the first statement, Genocchi explained:

> First of all, we must observe that Peru must not be blamed because only some of the authors of the atrocities are Peruvian, perhaps only a minority. A great number of the criminals are Colombians, Ecuadorians, Bolivians, English and citizens of other American and European nations. Furthermore, the Peruvian government, owing to the impossibility of communications with those very remote regions, and not from bad will or sheer neglect, has not been in a position to prevent the murder and the ill-treatment of the Indians. Everyone knows that the action of the government in the Putumayo is now being strengthened daily with more promptness and intelligent sacrifices. There is a need for more explicit laws to prohibit in Peru even a disguised slavery and the slave trade of the Indians. The Congress would certainly vote them through in order to find a remedy for a legislative deficiency, which in other times would be harmless, but which now has proven to be damaging. It impedes a vigorous intervention of the government and encourages the inhuman speculators.
>
> But what legislation was ever complete and perfect from the beginning? It is not just, therefore, to launch a general attack on the honor of Peru, without indicating those extenuating circumstances, which to the eyes of thoughtful people could rightly defend it. Furthermore, in this important question, one must always keep in mind a fact which slips by unnoticed: the grave international disputes, including wars, of which the region of the Putumayo was and is the object. That vast expanse, so rich in rubber, is a bone of contention between Peru, Ecuador and Colombia. The Peruvian government owns and defends it with weapons in hand. In such a state of affairs, how can it protect the unfortunate Indians whose oppressors avail themselves of the impunity that the uncertainty of the boundaries and the events of the guerilla warfare accord them?

"This reason," Genocchi concluded, "which constitutes an enormous difficulty for the Peruvian government, is often an insurmountable difficulty for the Church:"

> To which nationality must the bishop, to whom those territories would be assigned, belong? What would have to be the boundaries of the missions? Can one hope that the political jealousies cease, as they would have to, in view of the spiritual and material need of those people so worthy of compassion?

Concerning the second accusation, which assumed that the Pope was "guilty of complicity or at least of negligence in this serious state of affairs, so contrary to the Gospel and to humanity," Genocchi stated:

> It must be said at once that the author of the article is quite ignorant of the pressure brought to bear upon the Peruvian government by the Head of the Catholic Church, urging all possible measures against the continuance of such crimes. He is also unaware that Pius X was moved to tears by reports received about the massacre of the Indians by the rubber traders (who, as the British newspaper rightly says, were neither Catholic nor Protestants, but "godless men," devoid of all sentiments of humanity) and already did all he could through his representatives in South America. Moreover, he sent a special Visitor from Rome to collect all possible information in the area. His purpose was to put it at the disposal of the ecclesiastical authorities that they might present their case more forcibly for drastic action on the part of the government in favor of the oppressed Indians, "those beloved sons, poor and persecuted," as the Pope himself called them with tears. His Holiness has arranged for the establishing of new missions, and is doing everything possible, without counting any sort of sacrifice.
> The Daily News asks: "Why has not the Church made a public protest?" Because ordinarily it is not by clamor and noise that the best undertakings are initiated. Words are of no use when the situation demands a combined action of Church and government. When the Pope thinks it opportune, he will not fail to speak to the entire world in order to excite the generosity of Catholics, who must offer missionaries, Sisters, and money. In the meantime he is laboring to prepare the way for this great and necessary undertaking.[1]

* * *

After their two meetings Jerome suggested to Genocchi that they carry on a written exchange of views for confidential information of the British Legation and of the Apostolic Delegation. The reason for the exchange would be to prevent misunderstanding that could arise, given the fact that both of them would probably not be in Lima much longer. In a long letter of September 27, 1911, Jerome summarized the state of the Catholic missions in the interior of Peru and that of the Indian tribes under the various Prefects Apostolic. He also gave his own thoughts on the Catholic missions in the Putumayo.

The need for mission work in the Amazonian interior of South America could be taken for granted. "Two points remain," Jerome stated, "that of the existing missions and that of the reorganization of

---

[1] See also Genocchi's manuscript in ASV.DP. F.4. 195.

the same insofar as Peru is concerned." The existing missions were
those of San León de Amazonas, with headquarters at Iquitos; of San
Francisco de Ucayali, with headquarters at Contamana; and of Santo
Domingo de Urubamba, which had its headquarters at Cuzco.

They are under the supervision of the Apostolic Prefect. The first named
is served by Augustinians, the second by Franciscans, and the last named
by Dominicans. The number of missionaries in each prefecture is at
present, five at Iquitos, twenty in the Ucayali, and seven in the Urubamba
and Madre de Dios, the latter, as you informed me, to be soon increased
to ten or twelve. The funds at present available are what the Lima "Obra
de la Propagación de la Fé en el Oriente del Peru" have been able to
collect, and are entirely inadequate for the purpose. The subvention which
the Peruvian government has granted has not been paid.

The magnitude of the task can be understood by considering the
rivers flowing through the Apostolic Prefecture and by noting the
number of the Indian tribes.

In that of San Leon de Amazonas: the Caqueta, the Putumayo, the Napo,
the Tigre, the Pastaza, the Morona, the Paute, etc. In that of San
Francisco de Ucayali: the upper Maranon, the Huallaga, the Ucayali, the
Pachitea, the Javari, the Apurimac, etc. And in that of Santo Domingo
de Urubamba: the upper Purus, the Urubamba, the Madre de Dios, the
Inambari, the Tambopata, the Heath, etc. Altogether rivers which have
over seven thousand miles of water navigable for large steamers and as
many more for canoes and small craft.
The Indian tribes within the Prefectures Apostolic are in that of San
León: the Jivaros, Maynas, Roamaynas, Ticunas, Mayorunas, Chiribos,
Iquitos, Llamelos, Cocomas, Tutapiscos, Huitotos, Urarinas, Machinas,
Boras, Payquas, Cofanes, Canelos, Quixos, Curarayes, etc. In that of San
Francisco: Chamicoros, Cocamollas, Yaguanos, Conibos, Capanaguas,
Catuquinas, Sabetos, Panos and Sipopos Panos, Nahuas, Cachibo,
Remos, Amahuacas, Piros, Campas, Chunos, etc. In that of Santo
Domingo: Camaticas, Campas, Catongos, Sirineiris, Quichuas, Aymaras,
Pacacuaras, Hipurines, Guarayos, Tiromonos, etc.
Although there are other different languages, Quichuan is spoken
throughout the whole country, especially in the first two districts. In the
last named (Santo Domingo) Ayamara and Gurani may be the prevalent
tongues.

Father Izaguirre of the Franciscan Order was engaged in writing a full
history of the missions beginning with the time that these had been taken
over by the Order of Saint Francis from the Society of Jesus. "From a
study of this work, when it would become available, much would be
learned both as to causes of success and failure of the missions."

As for the reorganization, the English representative was aware that the ultimate decision would rest, of course, with the Congregation for the Propagation of the Faith.

> My esteemed colleague and friend and compatriot, Sir Roger Casement, is anxious to have an Irish mission in Iquitos and the Putumayo. The suitability of our countrymen for this field will have to be considered. Is not knowledge of Spanish and Spanish customs a sine qua non? The advantage of this idea would be the setting aside of this field as a special one for Hibernians, and once this may be decided on, then we can at once set about interesting Irishmen and Irishwomen in Ireland, the British Empire and the United States of America and securing their generous cooperation in funds.
>
> In any case, I would suggest that, of whatever nationality the mission or missionaries may be, I trust that they will be men who will join tact with zeal and who will be able to secure a maximum of assistance from the local authorities and a minimum of hostility from the traders. The priests chosen will have to face difficulties of all kinds, natural and artificial. My opinion is that the very *best* Fathers of all nationalities should be chosen by the Propaganda Fide. I would prefer the mission to be one of the Society of Jesus for the following reasons: they would have the necessary training, their absolute devotion is assured, no fear of the missionaries giving in, owing to apparent lack of success.

Father Leandro Cornejo, a Franciscan, told Jerome that the only practical plan was one which would permit the missionaries to take the place of the rubber traders. Though at first not opposed to this plan, on consideration Jerome was inclined to think that it would have to be adopted in a modified form. He understood that this plan had been successful with the Cayubaba Indians of the Mamore River at the mission of Exaltación in Bolivia.

In regard to the financial aspect of the missions, Peruvian help could not be counted on. Nevertheless, Jerome considered that there was something that could be done by the hierarchy.

> The Archbishop of Lima and the other bishops of Peru should organize throughout their dioceses conferences for the clergy and from the clergy to the laity as to the enormity of the crime of slavery and what national degradation it leads to. As Peru is exclusively reserved as a field for the Catholic Religion, it is quite incumbent on Catholics from every part of the world to provide the necessary funds, and I myself speaking as a Catholic, feel it is a case of our being tested and I trust that we may not be found wanting.

Genocchi would soon go to Iquitos and see that a decent church was urgently required. "The Peruvian central government, the department of Loreto, and the municipality of Iquitos *must* provide a respectable place for public worship." Jerome made the following suggestions:

> The Peruvian bishops should be asked at once to institute subscriptions for this purpose. A school for natives is required at Iquitos, one under the direction of Salesians, a headquarters building for the missionaries and headquarters also at Iquitos for nuns. I recall the admirable work done by the nuns in the Island of Haiti. A moving church should be obtained, I mean a river steamer which would accomodate a small party of missionaries that would be able to make use of the navigable rivers and which could be furnished with a movable altar and which also might be used as a hospital and should be furnished with the most urgently required remedies and surgical appliances.

At the conclusion of his letter, Jerome invited Genocchi to decide on a workable plan that could be put into practice. They might at present lack funds, but Jerome confided to Genocchi that while writing his letter he had by chance come across the following inspiring statement: "Saint Teresa said that Teresa with three pennies could accomplish nothing, but Teresa and her pennies, and Our Heavenly Father, could accomplish everything." Jerome was quite aware of the magnitude of the task, but considered it was a task worthy of the Catholic Church. He apologized to Genocchi if he had spoken too strongly on any point, but Genocchi was certainly aware of his feelings in the matter, and he rejoiced to think that the Holy Father had knowledge of the needs of the case.[2]

The following day, September 28, Genocchi replied with this letter:

> Dear Sir:
>
> To answer fully your request about Catholic missions for Peruvian Indians, I want to see one more of the religious Superiors dwelling in Lima. That will not happen until next Saturday.
>
> As the principal point in question is Iquitos with its immense province, I can tell you at the present time that five Augustinians of Iquitos are quite inadequate for the task, there being need of many missions throughout the Caucho region, and they remain in the city, where unfortunately they can do little or nothing. Iquitos should become the residence of a Catholic Bishop or of an Vicar Apostolic under whose direction missionaries of different Orders could work in different places. It seems not so difficult to obtain from the Peruvian government the

---

[2] L. Jerome to G. Genocchi, September 27, 1911. AGG. S.7/26.

erection of either a diocese or a Vicariate in Iquitos, with some additional allowances for the missionaries. Only, as you perfectly know, in view of the political agitation in Peru, we cannot trust to that but as to an eventual superaddition [sic]. I think, however, that funds can be provided elsewhere, except the living [expenses] of the Bishop, likely to be obtained from the government as well as from the other Bishops.

I am getting ready for my sea voyage to Iquitos, as I feel not strong enough to go by land. At my return I shall hopingly be able to express a more founded opinion on the matter and submit it to the Holy See. It is known how much His Holiness Pius X is interested in taking some practical steps soon to give help to those poor Indians of the Putumayo above all, and afterwards to those of the other provinces.

Let me avail myself of this occasion to express my gratitude to both the English government for favouring so actively the redemption of the Indians from every kind of slavery, and to you for your intelligent and hearty support given to me since the first time we met. I may sincerely say that without your information and kindness my preparation should not have reached half the way it did now.

    I remain,

Respectfully,

G. Genocchi [3]

The above letter shows with how calm a mind Genocchi could speak of the affairs of his mission and dispose things for his long journey to the upper regions of Peru. Yet only two days earlier, on September 26, he had received the saddest news that can fall to the lot of any son, especially one so far away: that of the death of his mother. It was a great sorrow, as his letters show, but the temperament of the man did not belie itself. Genocchi was not accustomed to making concessions to his personal feelings at the expense of his duty. He would not allow personal sorrow to disturb his apostolic undertaking. On the eve of setting out on his uncomfortable journey to his field of action, Iquitos, there were many and urgent things to be attended to. At the same time, his heart felt deeply for those distant sisters, left alone in life and without consolation. Still, he would sacrifice the demands of nature to those of his mission, not taking one hour from his duties of

---

[3] G. Genocchi to L. Jerome, September 28, 1911. PRO.FO. 45149. On October 5, 1911, L. Jerome sent to the Foreign Office his and Genocchi's letter with this comment: "I have the honour to enclose copies of letters I have exchanged with the Reverend Father G. Genocchi on the subject of Missions in the interior; together they form a short statement of the Missionary position and of the most pressing requirements. I made quite clear to Father Genocchi that what I wrote was in my private capacity as a Roman Catholic layman." PRO.FO. 45149.

the moment but awaiting the forced idleness of his boat trip to write home. It was on October 12 that he finally paid the debt to his heart with the following moving letter:

My dear sisters:

I am again at sea, and it will take a week to get to Panama. I sailed yesterday from Lima (which will still be my address), and only two days ago your letter of August 28 arrived, whereas the letter from Rome telling me of mother's death had reached me on September 26. I now realize that even if I had been in Rome, I would not have seen mother in her last moments, and that makes my being so far away less distressing. I am happy to learn that her death was without great pain. As for its suddenness, there is no reason to deplore that. She had prepared herself for it day and night. I am pleased that everything was done for her as it should be.

I spent all day of August 24, right through until 7 a.m. on the 25th (which in Italy would be noon of the 25th) in the train between Buenos Aires and Mendoza. I had one of the most disturbed nights in my life. Although I had a good berth in a sleeping-car, I could not close an eye and felt racked with fever without knowing why. I did nothing but think and pray right through the night and never before have my thoughts gone back to our house in Ravenna for so long a time and with such persistence. I did not feel up to saying Mass when we arrived at Mendoza, but still I did so, having a good rest in the afternoon and during the following night. After that I was quite well again. I attributed my insomnia during the night of the journey to some food I had in the car, yet the others who dined with me felt no disturbance. However that may be, it served to keep me awake and praying instead of sleeping while mother was on her deathbed.

What will Mariuccia do now, alone at Ravenna? I am wondering whether she will sell the house. In the meantime try to keep in good spirits and give a good example to everybody. Mariuccia has the merit of having helped poor mother for so many years, and we must indeed give her credit for that. We ourselves, on the other hand, have in different ways done what we could. It is for us now to go on with our duties, remaining united in perfect harmony so that mother's soul will be pleased with us.[4]

* * *

On October 6, Genocchi sent Cardinal Merry del Val the first information he had gathered on the state of the Indians in Peru. In the three or four weeks spent in Lima, he learned more than he could have

---

[4] G. Genocchi to his sisters, October 12, 1911. AGG. L.7/G.

hoped from clergymen and other experts, as well as from every sort of
document. He wrote as follows:

> Peru, with the exception of very few centers, is still a primitive country.
> Speaking only of Peru, the horrors committed by the rubber traders in
> the Putumayo which your Eminence certainly knows of (even from the
> two confidential reports of Consul Casement to Sir E. Grey, March 17
> and 21), are repeated, perhaps on a small scale, in the regions of the
> Ucayali and Urubamba. The poor Indians are put in chains, oppressed,
> massacred out of greed of greater gain and sometimes out of pure
> wickedness. An incalculable number of them perish in this manner. ...
> Even the Peruvian press is beginning to pay attention to the barbarities
> in the Putumayo, for some of which suit is being filed (they say *ad usum
> delphini*) in Iquitos. I am sending a document concerning it in the
> enclosed *La Prensa*. I wrote the article in reply in *El Bien Social* upon the
> advice of Msgr. Quattrocchi.

Genocchi related to the Holy See his observations concerning the
state of the missions, calling special attention to certain deficiences. In the
Urubamba the Dominicans seemed to work well, although some said that
they accomodated themselves somewhat to the abuses of the rubber
traders. However, the Apostolic Prefecture had few means because they
were totally separated from their religious Province in Peru. If the
Prefecture were united in some way with the wealthy Province, it could
expand and prosper. In the Ucayali, the *Descalzos*, exclusively Spanish and
very revered in Peru, were sacrificing themselves. The recent suppression
of their mission schools by order of the Superior General had greatly
affected and disheartened these zealous Franciscans. They might take
courage again if some appropriate satisfaction were obtained from Rome.
To this end, Genocchi considered writing about the *Descalzos* to the
Congregation for the Propagation of the Faith and to the Congregation
for Religious because they were doing a great deal of good among the
abandoned populations of the mountain area and among the Indians. The
Jesuits of Lima were willing to accept missions in those territories, but
they first wanted to be recognized by the government as were all other
religious congregations of Peru. This problem did not seem insurmountable to Genocchi.

The Redemptorists were doing immense good by traveling around
the country preaching missions. However, Genocchi pointed out:
"Many isolated pastors are taken to drunkenness and lust, acting as
implacable collectors of matrimonial and baptismal fees, and making
themselves hateful to those half-savage populations." Genocchi was
convinced that with more personnel supplied from Europe, even the
Redemptorists could take on a mission in Upper Peru without giving

up their profitable runs. They did not seem adverse to that. Genocchi
mentioned what he wrote in his preceding report of September 17
about the Assumptionists. If asked, they would devote themselves to
other missions besides those in Chile. In any case, Genocchi had no
doubt that, by establishing a Vicariate or a diocese in Iquitos, the Holy
See could find willing missionaries in Europe. The Holy Ghost Fathers
(who already had a school in Lima) were established not far from
Iquitos in Manaus, the Brazilian port of the Amazon River. They
assured Genocchi that they wished to establish a mission in the Upper
Peru as well, and in fact hoped to take the place of the Augustinians in
Iquitos. For this reason they had sent Father Kiefer to visit Iquitos and
the neighboring diocese of Chachapoyas during the previous year.
Genocchi ended his report with the following observation:

> What demands greater attention is some serious provision for Iquitos,
> where the few Augustinians are very much disliked. They do and can do
> almost nothing. The Prefect Apostolic of the mission, so-called de
> Amazonas, Father Paolino Diaz, is now in Europe, and will certainly come
> to Rome. I have heard that he wants to leave his prefecture, and to remove
> his religious because the hostility of the people and of the government
> render them impotent. Msgr. Quattrocchi is of the opinion that he should
> not be dissuaded too strongly from his purpose because that mission really
> needs another kind of worker, not so crushed and depressed.
> What is needed is a diocese or perhaps an Apostolic Vicariate with
> different religious orders to work not only in the city, which is already
> large and important, but also in the immense territory covered by the
> rubber traders. It will not be difficult to get along with the Peruvian
> government, especially if we await the change in the presidency next
> year. Now they have too many things to think about, and primarily
> about the elections.
> The new president will probably be Don Nicola Pierola, a well-balanced,
> broad-minded man, favorable to the Church's independence in Peru.
> Whoever the president may be, however, Msgr. Quattrocchi, a good
> judge of the milieu, and a friend of many present and future deputies,
> assures me that the government could obtain for Iquitos whatever the
> Holy See may desire.[5]

At his arrival in Lima, Genocchi found a letter waiting for him. It
was from Msgr. Bidwell and had been sent by Cardinal Merry del Val.
Genocchi delayed answering until October 7, 1911, since he did not
have sufficient information until then. He wrote to the Secretary of
State that after his imminent trip to Iquitos he would be able to answer

---

[5] G. Genocchi to Cardinal R. Merry del Val, October 6, 1911. ASV.SS. F.4. 70-73.

with more competence, but he did not think that he would have to change substantially what he was in a position to tell the Cardinal at that moment.

After considering the problem of what nationality the missionaries should be, Genocchi thought that the presence of English subjects would be a guarantee for the missionaries themselves and a safeguard for the Indians.

> There is certainly no greater difficulty for the Irish missionaries than for those of any other nation, with the exception, of course, of the bordering republics. Indeed the respect for, and the fear of, England which is felt here would be a good safeguard for them. Also, it should be noted that there are more than a few people who speak English in the area of Iquitos. The Irish missionaries, however, should never think that they could get along without the Spanish language. It is true that generally they have no inclination for foreign language, but I have also been acquainted with the good missionaries of Mill Hill and others who have overcome this obstacle.

As for the maintenance of the missionaries, Genocchi thought that an assured income of one pound per day (as from a capital of 10,000 pounds or a little more) was already an excellent guarantee for a small community which could also count on alms from Masses and on some special donations. Life in Iquitos was very expensive. Far from the city one could easily get some products from the soil. Genocchi closed his letter by saying that he would be able to tell better when he arrived in Iquitos.[6]

On November 13, 1911, Msgr. Bidwell passed on Genocchi's views to the Foreign Office in the following letter.

> Dear Mr. Drummond:
>
> The Information I have just received from Cardinal Merry del Val with reference to the proposed Putumayo Mission, is as follows: (1) If it is thought best that missionaries should be English or Irish, this will not give rise to difficulties with the local Ecclesiastical authorities. You will remember that Sir Roger Casement suggested that Irish missionaries should be sent out, as he thought it would be easier to raise funds in Ireland if this could be done. (2) The missionaries will be able to support themselves if they can count on a minimum income, from other than local sources, of 400 pounds sterling a year.

Bidwell added that the immediate question was how the money could be raised. Casement felt that the promises of the Peruvian government could not be relied upon too much. Bidwell had no doubt that he was right.[7]

---

[6] G. Genocchi to Cardinal R. Merry del Val, October 7, 1911. ASV.SS. F.4. 75-76.

[7] M. Bidwell to W. Drummond, November 13, 1911. PRO.FO. 45140.

CHAPTER VI

THE PUTUMAYO

After almost a month spent in Lima, Genocchi informed the Secretary of State that he was about to leave for Iquitos. Bearing in mind what Msgr. Sapinelli told him personally about Iquitos, what he had learned in Lima and the advice received from Msgr. Quattrocchi, he determined to go to Iquitos. Because the steamship of the Liverpool-Iquitos and New York-Iquitos line via the Amazon River passed through Barbados, he embarked for Barbados at Colon on October 24. This was the only possible route in that rainy season, unless he was willing to risk being stranded on the long and dangerous trip through the crags of the Andes. Should the Secretary of State have to send him orders by letter or by telegraph, the best means would always be the address of the Apostolic Delegation in Peru.[1]

The journey and the stay in Iquitos would not be easy. Genocchi was well aware of the danger that he might face. The possibility and the nature of these dangers can be seen in the following code that he left with the Apostolic Delegate in Lima before beginning his journey.

The first five numbers refer to the Augustinian Fathers in their relation with me:

1. Received warm welcome and lodging.
2. Received warm welcome but not lodging.
3. Received cold welcome, but they let me work.
4. Cold war.
5. Open war. It is necessary to send them orders by telegram.

The following numbers refer to my personal conditions of health:

....

13. I must leave Iquitos soon for reason of health.
14. I have become seriously ill.
15. My serious sickness has become grave.
16. There is no hope that I will recover.[2]

---

[1] G. Genocchi to Cardinal R. Merry del Val, October 6, 1911. ASV.SS. F.4. 70.
[2] ASV.DP. F.4. 213.

Genocchi left Lima on October 10, two weeks earlier than planned. In a letter, written on the ship *Guatemala*, dated "one day out of Lima and heading North, October 11, 1911," Genocchi sent details of his mission and expressed his feelings and expectation regarding his journey to the capital of the Putumayo.

> Yesterday I departed for Panama, where I shall arrive on the sixteenth. I shall cross the Isthmus by train and after eight days will enter the Atlantic to go to Brazil and more precisely to Belém do Pará, near the mouth of the Amazon River. There I shall embark again and proceed up the river for more than 2,000 miles, in order to reach Iquitos and beyond, where the rubber traders have committed, and to this day continue to commit, the most incredible cruelty, including murdering the Indians by thousands, with the result that some tribes have been exterminated. It is there that the Church must accomplish its work of setting up good mission centers which will be a check on the inhuman rubber traders as well as the health of the surviving Indians.
>
> From Iquitos, which is a large city, after seeking to set up whatever is possible for those deserted Catholics and after preparing a plan for the mission among the Indians, I will return to Lima to confer again with the Apostolic Delegate and also with the Peruvian government which is well disposed toward us. I have spoken with the Minister of Foreign Affairs, and he gave me letters of introduction. I trust much more in the introduction of the English government, which concerns itself with my mission as if it were its own and sends instructions to its consuls and representatives to support me....
>
> And from now onward, by the mercy of God, even if I must die in this country, where contagious diseases abound, I will have the awareness of having done my duty and nothing more. The Lord has given me the grace to understand well the parable of the talents and that of the servant who after having worked in the field must still serve at the master's table. I am well convinced of the truth of *servi inutiles sumus*—We are useless servants.[3]

In another letter, written on the same ship, dated "three days out of Lima and heading North, October 13, 1911," after recalling briefly the massacre of the Indians, he shows great concern for the necessity of the intervention of the Church, despite the difficulties.

> I am at sea on my way to... Upper Peru. That is where, more than anywhere else, they massacre the poor Indians whom they have reduced to slavery, compelling them to gather rubber for speculators. There we must establish good missions to save these unhappy people and prevent their complete destruction. The great difficulties, diseases and dangers of

---

[3] G. Genocchi to Cardinal A. Capecelatro, October 11, 1911. AGG. L.3/C.

every kind which prevail in these parts, are certainly no obstacles as far as missionaries and sisters are concerned; they are even an attraction.[4]

After six day's sailing, Genocchi disembarked from the *Guatemala* at Panama, crossed the isthmus (which was not yet cut) by train and arrived at Colon, on the Atlantic coast. On October 24 he left for Barbados, the farthest island of the Eastern Antilles. This island was linked with the story of the atrocities in Putumayo because Barbados was a British possession and caused the direct intervention of England in the affairs with which the Holy See was concerned.

An Indian boy was on board the British ship Genocchi traveled on from Colon to Cartagena. He was about twelve years of age and had been bought by a Colombian lady in the outskirts of Panama for one dollar and twenty cents. She was bringing him to Colombia where undoubtedly she would be able to do whatever she wanted with him. Genocchi tried unsuccessfully to speak with the boy. He was aware that the mistress did not approve of his attempts. However, it seemed that she cared for the boy. Genocchi hoped that it was not simply because of the circumstances imposed by being aboard an English steamship. "This is one of the thousands of facts," Genocchi remarked, "which proves the persistence of the ancient practice of slaveholding in these countries." [5]

From Barbados to Belém do Pará, Genocchi was on a narrow steamship which was designed more for freight than for passengers. He traveled with Peruvian soldiers who had been treated in Barbados for illnesses contracted in the skirmishes of the Coquetá against Bolivia. The sea was calm and Genocchi was able to listen to and take part in their conversation. They confirmed the fact that the Indians were subject to dreadful barbarities. In his report to the Secretary of State Genocchi drew the conclusion that in Peru and bordering countries traffic in human flesh was not regarded as a greater crime than smuggling contraband goods in Europe.

> The exploitation of the Indians, reduced to slavery, is horribly barbaric, as we know, but it makes little impression on either the Peruvians or their neighboring peoples. Coercion and the whip are necessary with the Indians, else nothing can be obtained from them: this is the principle. To buy them, to sell them or catch them as you can, is regarded as no greater fault than the smuggling of goods in Europe.[6]

---

[4] G. Genocchi to L. Carbone, October 13, 1911. AGG. L.3/C.
[5] G. Genocchi to Cardinal R. Merry del Val, November 12, 1911. ASV.SS. F.4. 77.
[6] G. Genocchi to Cardinal R. Merry del Val, November 12, 1911. ASV.SS. F.4. 77.

On November 12, Genocchi arrived at Belém do Pará on the mouth of the Amazon River. This was the main center of the rubber trade. Genocchi was a guest of the Archbishop while he waited for a steamship to Iquitos which was due in two weeks. The following day the English ship *Ucayali* was leaving, but it was already full. The English consul promised to arrange somehow to have a place for Genocchi who was willing to sleep on deck if necessary, in order to save two precious weeks. However, he could not be assured of having a place until a few moments before departure. In the meantime he sent his sixth report to the Secretary of State because he was not certain that he would have time to write on the following day. After having informed him of his arrival at Belém do Pará, Genocchi continued as follows:

> Iquitos should become a missionary center and residence for an Ordinary or an Vicar Apostolic. The Peruvian government, as I already wrote to your Eminence, is favorable, and both the men and the money will be found. No religion exists there at all. I shall look into it better, and I shall do as I can to awaken the Christian spirit in a small nucleus and then I shall report to your Eminence.

In the meantime a doubt arose about travel plans. Genocchi thought it was best to bring it to the attention of the Secretary of State in order to avoid excessive expenses. Once he had conscientiously finished his work in Iquitos, he would pass by Belém do Pará again. Would it really be worth the trouble to return to Lima, which would take about a month of travel, when he was only ten days away from Lisbon? If the Holy See thought it was necessary, he was, of course, ready to do so. On his return to Belém do Pará he would telegraph, saying as much as would be necessary. The Secretary of State could answer at the home of the Archbishop of Belém do Pará.[7]

The following day the boat was fully booked and no berth was available.

> November 13. My hopes were in vain. The steamship which was leaving yesterday had its places all taken from New York and there was no way possible to get a seat, not even on the deck. I shall have to wait here another two weeks. With the very kind Archbishop and other persons I am looking to see if another way out can be found.[8]

Genocchi was told that there would be another boat in a fortnight but when it came, once again there were no berths. However, Genocchi

---

[7] G. Genocchi to Cardinal R. Merry del Val, November 12, 1911. ASV.SS. F.4. 77.

[8] G. Genocchi to Cardinal R. Merry del Val, November 12, 1911. ASV.SS. F.4. 78.

was allowed to board provided he was willing to make the trip without a cabin or berth. He accepted and under these conditions took the long and tiring river trip which lasted a little less than a month.

The vast sluggish waters of the Amazon River flow out into the Atlantic through an estuary hundreds of miles wide, from the mountains of Ecuador and Peru across the continent. The steamer had to cover nearly a thousand miles before reaching the river junction at Manaus, where at last the Amazon begins to assume the proportions of a river rather than of an ever flowing lake. The confluence of one great tributary after another was passed on the way as they steamed on under a broiling sun, through the endless expanse of swamps, forest and luxuriant undergrowth. It was scarcely conceivable that human beings could survive for long in the forest and swamps scattered through hundreds of square miles of low-lying country, continually flooded in the rainy seasons. Swarms of mosquitoes and sandflies made it impossible for even the most hardy Indian race to live there. In a letter addressed to his friend, Levi della Vida, Genocchi described how he passed the time during the long journey:

> George, I have never been bored. In the long journey up the Amazon River, I had no bed nor even a corner to retire to. Some mornings I could not even wash my face, after having slept fully clothed amidst all kinds of people. But I did not get upset because of this. I made little of the needs of my body and I immersed myself in reading. Imagine, I reread all of Dante's Divine Comedy, some cantos more than once. Then I began to speak with Spaniards or Englishmen, and so I passed my days between enlightening conversations and readings.[9]

On December 23, Genocchi arrived at Iquitos. The city was infested with yellow fever which the locals called the *patriotic* fever because it killed a great number of unwelcome foreigners. Some twenty Spaniards arrived in November. No one survived. Two robust men and one woman, who had traveled with Genocchi and whom he knew very well, died within days of their arrival. Genocchi wrote:

> There has been an extraordinary outbreak of the disease, due to the dry spell. I was not anxious about it but took care of myself and was in no way affected by it. Until now Our Lord has preserved me from all such dangers; but, in any case, by his grace, fear of death could not make me deviate from the line of duty. I am careful, take what precautions I can, and then on with my work. ... Should God wish to call me to the next life from here, it would be, I admit it, one further sacrifice but what of

---

[9] G. Genocchi to Giorgio Levi della Vida, January 28, 1912. AGG. L.10/L.

that? Were I to sacrifice myself a hundred times more than the little I do, I would still have to recall those words of the Gospel: *"Quando feceritis haec omnia dicite: servi inutiles sumus"* [When you have done all that is commanded you, say, "We are unworthy servants." Lk. 17:10]. Of course one must not only say that, but believe it; otherwise it would be hypocrisy. Look up in the Gospel that beautiful passage, which on the surface seems even inhuman and devoid of feeling. ... Above all, I am content to suffer because I do so in order to obey Our Lord and the Holy Father, which is the same thing.[10]

On January 2, 1912, Genocchi informed Cardinal Merry del Val of his arrival at the capital of the Putumayo. After what he termed "an exceptionally rapid journey" along the Amazon River, Genocchi was received very amiably by the new Prefect Apostolic, Father Pedro Prat, and by his confrere, Father Laurentino Alvarez. With the two missionaries Genocchi found the ex-Prefect Apostolic of the Ucayali, Father Agostino Alemany. He had lost an eye and was on the way to Lima to be treated.[11]

* * *

Iquitos was an observation post. For fifty days, from December 23 to February 11, Genocchi devoted himself with his usual energy to the most urgent part of his mission. His task had been simplified to a great extent by the diligence with which he had gathered all the necessary information from the first moment of his landing in South America. With the information which Genocchi received from Jerome in Lima, he was well aware of the situation of the Indians of the Putumayo and of the Anglo-Peruvian Rubber Company's responsibility for the crimes against these Indians. Among his notes are five pages taken from Roger Casement's report to Sir Edward Grey dated March 17, 1911. These pages contain geographical and historical information about the Putumayo and a precise account of the system of torture and killing used by the rubber traders.

Around 1886 the Colombian *conquistadores*, Crisostomo Hernandez and Benjamin Larranaga, entered the territory in search of rubber and won the natives with small gifts. The *conquistadores* brought with them the peons whom they called *racionales* to distinguish them from the Indians whom they called *irracionales*. The peons first used kindness to induce the natives to work and then turned to force. The chief of the

---

[10] G. Genocchi to T. Mantrici, March 4, 1912. AGG. L.11/M.
[11] G. Genocchi to Cardinal R. Merry del Val, January 2, 1912. ASV.SS. F.4. 85-86.

Indians compelled his tribe to cooperate and the Indians submitted with docility. In 1896, the Arana Brothers Company of Peru decided to establish their headquarters in the nearby city of Iquitos to provide the rubber traders with food and supplies. The Company quickly took over nearly all the posts of the Colombian rubber traders because of the extraordinary rubber-producing capacity of the area. In 1905, Julio Cesar Arana went to England to interest some London gentlemen in the Arana Brothers holdings. He succeeded, and on October 1, 1907, the Peruvian Amazon Rubber Company, Ltd., was formed.

On obtaining possession of a tract of land, the rubber trader considered it to be his own in the strictest sense of the word. He spoke of it as his, referred to "my Indians," and "my river," treating as pirates any strangers who dared to trespass on his property. "Rubber pirates" were shot on sight, while "thefts" of Indians involved bloody reprisals. An Indian tribe that one "conquered" became the exclusive property of the successful assailant, and this lawless claim was recognized as a right. The civil authorities were in effect too far away to put an end to this custom, sanctioned by long tradition and the conviction that "Indians have no rights." Very often government employees shared the same conviction and actively intervened to capture runaway Indians to return them to the bondage from which they had fled.

Every station had its *muchachos*, young Indians taken from one tribe and used for acts of terror in other districts. *Cholitos* or *Indiecitos* were small Indian boys (possibly orphans) taken and trained in cruelty by the rubber traders who armed them and incited their basest instinct. They lived in the so-called "Indians' houses." In 1910, La Chorrera, the principal station, had 101 salaried *racionales* and some 200 *muchachos* scattered among ten stations. The duty of flogging was ordinarily imposed upon the *racionales* and the *muchachos*. A black Colombian, Simon Angulo, took particular delight in the job and knew how to draw blood with each stroke. Nearly ninety per cent of the Indians who were forced by the whites to work at rubber-gathering, bore deep scars from blows received.

Ordinarily for the crime of attempting to escape, torture and death occurred after flogging. Water plus salt and vinegar were rubbed into the wounds as remedies for the flogging. However, flogging might be the least of the tortures inflicted. Often suffering was aggravated by stocks. The hungry Indians who were put in the stocks ended up by scraping away the filth and eating it or by eating the worms that infected their own wounds. They were left for days, weeks, and even months in the stocks with their legs squeezed into the holes between two heavy and impossible-to-move girders. Those whose flesh turned putrid in the stocks were killed as incurable or as a possible source of disease for others. The victims in the stocks — men, women, children, and at times entire families — were exposed to the worst abominations.

Untold tortures included tying a man to a huge upright beam and suddenly letting him fall or hanging a man by the neck, his feet off the ground. The victim was released only when he was at the point of dying with his tongue hanging out. A Peruvian named Fidel Velarde invented the torture of tying the victim's hands behind his back and holding him under water until he was almost at the point of suffocation. Aquileo Torres, a Colombian-appointed warder, amused himself by cutting the ears off the Indians before murdering them. Alfredo Zegana did the same even up to 1910. The brothers Aurelio and Arístide Rodriguez, who were superintendents of two districts, massacred several hundred Indians. Philomeno Vasquez, after hunting down Indians in a long series of raids, boasted that he had left the road "a pretty sight indeed." Aguero had a harem of eleven women; he raped others at will. All the *racionales* had women, but these women were not the wives of living Indians, because the husbands prefered to be killed rather than work for the company. In fact, several were killed for this very reason.

With a load as much as 140 pounds each and chained in a long file, the Indians had to carry rubber from the secondary station to La Chorrera, a distance of about forty miles. For food they had nothing except roots and plants gathered here and there through the journey by their own little children, to save them from starving. Mothers with very small children were able to carry little and were consequently beaten.

Casement declared that if the killings continued at this rate, there would be no more Indians in the Putumayo within ten years. A Peruvian replied, "Not ten, but six years." Meanwhile the system assured the civilized world of a million pounds of rubber each year from the Putumayo (1,289,000 pounds in 1906).[12]

Genocchi recorded further information from a book, *Montañas De Ayacucho y Alto Ucayali*, by Pedro Portillo who was formerly the civil Prefect of Iquitos. The author spoke of the atrocities carried on by the white people and of the human flesh markets in those territories. He concluded by saying: "It is best to remain silent until the government can act more rapidly upon those despicable men who know no other law than that of profit and pleasure." And a bit further on he added:

> Our natives were few and they are disappearing. The tribes attack and
> destroy each other. Infanticide reigns. Children and women, the spoils of

---

[12] AGG. S.7/12.

war, are sold. The present rubber traders of the Ucayali and other rivers go there, not to build families and prosperity, but to obtain riches and Peruvian slaves, to exchange them for pounds sterling. ... For every Chinese man who enters, ten, twenty or thirty Peruvian Indians are sold abroad.[13]

Such was the situation in the Putumayo at the time of Genocchi's arrival. Additional documentation, which Genocchi gathered on his own during his stay in Iquitos, further confirmed the inhuman treatment of the Indians.

* * *

On his arrival, Genocchi was immediately struck by the sight of innumerable small Indian boys, generally with cropped hair, who were trained to do the white man's bidding. Father Laurentino gave an example of how the trade in Indian boys might occur. "About four months ago," the missionary explained, "a well-known merchant who wanted to sell a *cholita* (sic) for fifty pounds came to Iquitos. He then offered it for forty pounds to the Ferrant Company. Finally he ceded it to a Company to which he owed thirty pounds."[14] In his diary Genocchi recorded that there were few families who did not have these boys and especially girls of the Indian tribes at their service. This occurred even under the eyes of the authorities. It was true that most of these unfortunate ones became accustomed to their condition, resigning themselves to their situation. "There were especially plenty of girls who seldom fled the lust of their masters and masters' sons, who from the time they were children believed that every desire was permitted to them."[15]

Genocchi's first source of information came from the Augustinian Fathers who gave him lodging. Following a conversation with the ex-Prefect Apostolic of Ucayali, Genocchi wrote as follows:

Father Alemany tells me about the traffic in human flesh carried on by Antonio Vasana, a Spaniard, a fugitive from Ceuta: hundreds and thousands of women and children. This criminal keeps going further inland into the upper Ucayali and eludes all searches. Most corrupt authority! ... Among other things, Father Alemany impressed upon me that, while traveling with his confrere Father Cornejo four or five years

[13] AGG. S.7/23. See Pedro Portillo, *Montanas de Ayacucho y Alto Ucayali*, (Lima, 1901), p. 53.

[14] AGG. S.7/16. *Cholita* or *Cholata* (Genocchi's manuscript is not very legible) is not found in the Spanish dictionary. Probably it means a group of *cholitos* (Indian boys).

[15] G. Genocchi to Cardinal R. Merry del Val, March 29, 1912. ASV.SS. F.4. 103.

ago, he was on a steamboat full of Indian girls from eight to sixteen years of age. They were all sold to a Jewish man and probably brought to Europe. The priest could do nothing to prevent it.[16]

From the same missionary, Genocchi learned of a report concerning the upper Peruvian regions. It was dated August 27, 1907, and had been sent to the Minister of Justice of Peru, Dr. Charles W. Washbourne. He drew the attention of the Supreme government to what he termed "the infamous trade in buying and selling boys and girls which for years has been practiced in parts of the forest region, in spite of the repeated prohibitions of the government, as if those poor natives were irrational beings, or, to be still more blunt, as if they were sheep or horses." This trade increased the hunting of those Indians so frequently indulged in; they were seized in their houses in the moment when they least expected it. Father Alemany could cite many examples to confirm his statement. He limited himself to refer only to the one case which took place the preceding year:

> The Campas Indians of Ubiriqui River were dwelling peacefully in their houses when suddenly there fell upon them men sent on a slave raid by one of the traders of the upper Ucayali who lives near Unini. These, without warning, attacked the innocent Campas, seizing those whom they could, killing many men so that few escaped their cruelties. Even up to now the number of their victims is not known. It is certain that many were found in a state of decomposition. All the houses of the Ubiriqui were burnt.

These deeds had exasperated the Indians. Father Alemany warned: "If no effective remedy is applied, later on we shall not be safe even in the mission village, nor shall we be able to continue to win over and civilize the natives who dwell in our forests." [17]

Father Prat passed on to Genocchi a letter which he had received from Father Carrasco. In the letter Father Carrasco related that Decio Guzman's people had gone to conduct a slave raid in the Yalma River, on the pretext that certain Yalma Indians had not paid him in full for some goods. They were able to take only four men and six women with their children. They sent the women and children ahead in a canoe down the river. The four prisoners were on a balsa guarded by five men. One night, when everyone was sleeping, a Yalma Indian freed himself and the others and together they killed the five guards. Father Carrasco commented:

---

[16] AGG. S.7/25.
[17] AGG. S.7/25.

They should never have gone to such extreme measures of revenge, but
if you keep in mind that the guards had burned their houses, stolen their
plantations, thrown their beds, knives and swords into ditches ... and
had left the prisoners with only what they had on and furthermore sent
their women ahead, God knows for what purpose, I think they should
be excused. These Yalmas have returned to us and demanded their
women and children. ... Guzman, having passed by here, made us
understand that he intends to bring as many Yalmas, Ticuans and
Witotos as he can to the Purus River. Father, see if you can bring about
the liberation of the aforesaid women and children."

The letter included the following postscript:

Guzman and his people were taken prisoners while they were about to
cross the Putumayo border in the direction of the Purus River. Final
news item: Guzman brothers had been engaged in transporting fifty
Indian families. Hence the arrest.[18]

On September 8, 1907, Father Prat had also informed the Minister
of Justice about the difficulties encountered by the missionaries. He and
Father Placido Mallo were appointed to the mission of Pebas which lies
only a few hours' distance from Iquitos. In their work they obtained
scanty results because of the opposition of the rubber traders who were
interested that the Indians should remain "in the grossest ignorance (*en
la más crasa ignorancia*)" in order to exploit them with great ease. Along
the Putumayo River it was impossible to establish any mission owing to
the abuses of the rubber traders against the Indians whom they
"maltreated and murdered for no reason (*por motivos frívolos*), seizing
their women and children." In another report, dated August 27, 1907,
Father Prat spoke of slave raids and massacres everywhere. "After such
reports," Genocchi asks in his notes, "what did Peru's Minister of
Justice do? It is no wonder that the massacred and tortured Indians
committed some crimes against the whites." [19]

The last document found in Genocchi's diary concerning the
slavery of the Indians in the Putumayo is the Pastoral letter of Father
Paulino Diaz. The letter is dated September 10, 1902, when Father Diaz
was the Prefect Apostolic in Iquitos:

There is a larger number of native people in the Amazonic region, who
are descendants of some of the tribes civilized by the Spanish missionaries. ... They have been almost completely exterminated by the
greed and avarice of the white rubber traders who, taking advantage of

---

[18] AGG. S.7/25.
[19] AGG. S.7/11.

the apathy and benevolence of the Indians and using as an excuse that
they owe money, ... are able to subject them to a true slavery. Like slaves
who were taken from Brazil, Bolivia ... dying of starvation and sickness,
sold as I have told you. ... The owner has all power over them ... trading
in human flesh even though they consider themselves civilized and in
spite of the efforts with which some of the local authorities have tried to
abolish this horrible trade. ... Another more horrible mode of slavery, if
this is possible, is that almost every household in this Amazonic region is
made up of slaves bought from the natives by men without conscience,
including Europeans, or taken by force from their families by hunting
them as if they were animals." [20]

Genocchi also contacted the civil authorities. He informed the
Secretary of State that "having brought [with him] letters recom-
mending [him] to both official and unofficial, Catholic and heterodox
personages, [he had] already obtained quite a bit of new information."
He stated: "With my own eyes I have seen other things, and I shall see
and learn still more, since I do not have to leave here until the end of
January or perhaps even later if the steamship which I am counting on
does not arrive in time." [21] For the most part there is nothing explicitly
stated in Genocchi's notes about his encounters with the civil authorities. However, there are several hints in Genocchi's reports about the
authorities conniving with the criminals and about their *political* attitude
towards the Holy See.

The main concern of Genocchi in his dealing with local authorities
was the decision taken by the Peruvian government on April 13, 1907,
concerning the ecclesiastical jurisdiction of Iquitos. Genocchi recorded
the decree of the government in his notes:

Considering that the Apostolic Prefecture has as an object the infidels ...
and not the civilized people; that the Apostolic Prefecture has given the
indicated interpretation by order of the diocesan administration of
Chachapoyas ... according to the information gathered from the Section
of Cult and to what was ordered by the attorney of the Supreme Court,
we resolve:

1. that the jurisdiction of the Apostolic Prefecture covers only the
uncivilized territories and in no case should it cover the civilized
territories, which are under the jurisdiction of the respective diocese and
of the other authorities who constitute the ecclesiastical hierarchy;

---

[20] AGG. S.7/16. See also *España y América*, 1 (1903), p. 516, 517; and Genocchi's
letter to Cardinal R. Merry del Val, March 29, 1912. ASV.SS. F.4. 103.
[21] G. Genocchi to Cardinal R. Merry del Val, January 2, 1912. ASV.SS. F.4. 85.

2. that the parish of Iquitos does not belong to the Apostolic Prefecture of San Leon de Amazonas but to the Diocese of Chachapoyas and it is under the jurisdiction of that Ordinary;

3. to suggest to the Bishop of Chachapoyas to transfer Father Pedro Correra to the parish of Iquitos and to notify the Minister of Cult of this change.

(signed)
Charles W. Washbourne [22]

This had been a unilateral act against the Presidential decree which was issued on October 27, 1898, with the assent and approbation of the Holy See. The Congregation for the Propagation of the Faith on April 24, 1907, had declared "the entire Department of Loreto [the capital of which was Iquitos] to be under the Prefecture of San León de Amazonas, and the Department of San Martín to be under the bishop of Chachapoyas." After his contact with the local authority, Genocchi was in a position to communicate only the following information to the Secretary of State:

> The municipal authorities and the governmental authorities avail them selves of this decision [i.e., the decree of April 13, 1907], when it serves their own interests. However, they could create greater inconveniences than they do. This apparent friendliness of the government did not please the Freemasons and other leaders of Iquitos, but they now remain silent because they know that the government does not wish to put the Holy See off too much. ... Several of them, with whom I am in contact, due purely to the duty of courtesy, have said it to me. I do not know, however, if this is a bribe with which the government is trying to keep their mouths shut cheaply, or if the government is really meditating spite against the Holy See as soon as it can. At any rate, elections are approaching with their respective machinations and possible revolutions, and everything will depend on the new government. The new President will not take office before September. [23]

* * *

Genocchi did not limit his inquiry to the officials. He also contacted people who were either directly or indirectly involved in the enslavement of Indians and the atrocities committed against them. Genocchi recorded that one day he met an "old and kind trader" who

---

[22] AGG. S.7/21.
[23] G. Genocchi to Cardinal R. Merry del Val, February 9, 1912. ASV.SS. F.4. 87-88.

spent many years in the Ucayali and who was at that time working on board the *Atahualpa*:

> He disapproves of the barbarities of so many. He relates, however, that with sixty Indians he enlisted with other whitemen he fought an *indiata* which was molesting the travellers. They remained hidden until about 2 a.m., when the dance in the village ended; then they approached. A boy noticed them, sounded the alarm and the Indians fled. The attacking band killed some, took seven boys and girls and **gave** [Genocchi's emphasis] them to their own sixty Indians who took them as slaves.[24]

On January 12, Genocchi received a visit from a certain Fidel Bao who was captain of a launch. He was a Spaniard who had become a naturalized Peruvian. Genocchi writes:

> This evening Fidel Bao came to see me. We spoke about the uprising of the Campas Indians who have killed whites and half-castes. He knows these people well and tell me that they were particularly embittered because some whites had kidnapped their sons and daughters and sold them. Boys were sold for up to thirty pounds in the presence of their parents. The government sent soldiers to punish these poor Indians, but they were not afraid because they had a refuge inaccessible to the whites together with a large supply of ammunition for their guns.[25]

A week later, on January 19, Fidel Bao once again visited Genocchi and filled him in with additional information:

> A seaman of the launch who took an orange from the orchard of Manuel Reategni escaped a rifle bullet only by sheer miracle. This Manuel Reategni, an old man living in Iquitos, was rich and a great scourge of the Indians. Three times he succeeded in avoiding trial by means of money. The fourth time he tried in vain because he found an incorruptible judge. He had a stone house, which served as a harem, with fifty women or more living under strict rule and kept for lust and for market. He had a large cage on his grounds in which he kept a tiger. A houseboy who did not come immediately when called was thrown into the cage before his father's eyes. The father was threatened with a gun when he fell on his knees to beg for mercy.[26]

On February 5, Genocchi recorded that El Duque of Caballococha came to tell him of three Indians "who had been disembowelled quite nearby." After that we find in Genocchi's diary an account of a

---

[24] AGG. S.7/15.

[25] V. Ceresi, *Op. Cit.*, p. 456.

[26] AGG. S.7/15.

A side street at Iquitos

horrifying episode which demonstrates to what extremes of vengeance and barbarism the poor Indians were driven by the white men's ferocity. "A white woman in Iquitos was condemned by the Indians to eat the fingers of her husband whom they ate alive, cutting him into small pieces. While the Indians were drunk and asleep, she was able to flee." [27]

* * *

Among Genocchi's papers were two documents which he identified as **A** and **B**. They serve to prove the responsibility of the government employees. In the first of these documents Genocchi cited from *La Felpa* (Iquitos, December 29, 1907) the list of Indians killed as reported and signed by Rinaldo Torres during his session at Antenas:

> The *muchachos* Pimenta, Pedro Cutildo, Felice Santiago, and Satanas were sent to slaughter them by Elias Martinengui in March, 1903. Those who did not obey the orders of the Captain had to be put to death at once (Here the names of seven Indians follow which we do not think it prudent to publish. Also the names of two women). Of the Guilomos tribe, two Indians; of the Huchalias, seven Indians and one woman, Maria, wife of B.; the Captain not satisfied with ordering her scourged, introduced a stick into her vagina; of the Nyenes tribe, four Indians. In Abyssinia the same Aguero took an Indian out of the prison and shot him twice. This was Captain P. In Cahuinari J. M. was killed by Carlos Miranda. And there are others about whom I will tell afterwards. These crimes were witnessed by R. T., F. T., I. M. A., P. B.. These persons can testify wherever it may be needed that the only reason these crimes were committed was not on account of any transgression, but in order to steal. Total killed: 25.

Genocchi noted that "the Indians of the Putumayo were relatively happy with Calderón, Larranaga, and other former rubber traders, until the Arana Company arrived with people like Normand, Aguero, the two Rodriguez brothers, and José Fonseca. Fonseca even in 1912 simply laughed at the police who sought him along the borders of Brazil and Peru." From the same newspaper Genocchi quoted an account of the treatment that the Indians suffered at the hands of these people:

> They imposed on each Indian the obligation to collect five *arrobas* [i.e., 125 pounds] every fifteen days. The Indian who did not bring enough was thrown to the ground to await a flogging or a bullet or the *machete* at the verdict of the captain. The captain ordinarily gives fifty lashes with scourges until the flesh drops from his body in strips, or else orders

---

[27] AGG. S.7/25, 15.

him to be cut to pieces with a *machete* — and this in the presence of the women and children, his own or those of others. When the Indians deliver the full amount required from them, they are usually given some object worth about thirty or fifty *centavos* (a mouth-organ, colored cotton handkerchief, a few beads or similar trash) and they are overjoyed, chiefly at having escaped a flogging. There used to be 20,000 of them. They have been reduced to half that number. As a result, the traders oblige the women to work, and they are ill-treated just as the men.[28]

In document **B** Genocchi cited evidence found in two distinct sources. The first was once again that of Torres presented in *La Sancion* (Iquitos, November 19, 1907):

> Rinaldo Torres writes of twenty-five Indians killed in 1907 by order of Victor Macedo, Jacobo Barchilon and Rafel Laraniaga. Aristide Rodriguez denounced them, but they paid half a million soles and were able to escape. Torres was an eyewitness.

The second source was an article signed and attested to under oath by M. G. for *La Felpa* (Iquitos, January 11, 1908):

> The Indian is so humble that when he sees that the needle of the scale does not mark twenty-five pounds, he himself stretches out his hands and throws himself on the ground ready to receive his punishment. Then the captain or one of his subalterns bends down, takes the Indian by his hair, strikes him, raises his head, drops it face downwards on the ground, and the face is beaten and kicked and covered with blood, and the Indian is scourged. This is when they treat them best, for at other times they cut them to pieces with a machete. At Matanzas I saw Indians being tied to a tree, their feet above the ground. Afterwards the persecutors would put wood under their feet and burn them alive. This they did for sheer amusement. M.G.

In closing his report, Genocchi called attention to the conclusion of the newspaper's editor, Saldana Rocca: "During the five months I have been denouncing the crimes of the Putumayo, I have not been called upon to give evidence under oath. In the meantime the crimes remain unpunished and the victims still suffer."[29]

Following the Foreign Office's confidential notification of the result of Casement's inquiry, the Peruvian government had sent a representative to conduct a further investigation. Genocchi reported a notice from *La Prensa* (Lima, September 21, 1911, *Ed. de la tarde*) that

---

[28] AGG. S.7/18.
[29] AGG. S.7/19.

Judge Rómulo Paredes had returned from the Putumayo with documents and articles (chests of oxidized human bones and chains with traces of blood) and that Aurelio Rodriguez, to whom more than 500 murders have been attributed, had been arrested. He added immediately the cynical comment from an editorial in *El Heraldo* of Iquitos: "the government officials, both political and judicial, should ignore the problem since Peru received a vast amount of land from the Arana Company, more than they could have dreamed of." [30]

Genocchi wrote at this time to Filippo Tolli, President of the Italian Anti-slavery Society: "The search for rubber, which is here called black gold, has given rise to worse abuses in these districts than in the Congo." He went on to add:

> In some parts of South America, in spite of the laws, the most shameful slavery prevails, with massacres, sales, atrocious tortures, and every other iniquity of which brutalized and degenerate man is capable when he is free from the control of law.

Catholic missions, the only possible deterrent to the wholesale destruction of the Indians, were lacking where they were most urgently needed. Genocchi concluded: "For this the Holy Father wishes to make provision and the idea is worthy of the highest praise." [31]

At the end of his investigation Genocchi acquainted Cardinal Merry del Val with what he had seen with his own eyes.

> Crimes against the poor Indians continue. They are kidnapped, sold and murdered. It is true, the situation is not as bad as before, but it still exists to a small extent. ... There are very recent facts which occurred during my stay in Iquitos, for which I have the best proof. I have manifested some to the English Consul who was unaware of them. I am keeping records and do not think it necessary to make specific reference in this letter, the matters being ones that Your Eminence has heard and read many times. I shall say only that a few days ago the raid of a rubber trader called Decio Guzman ruined the mission of the Augustinians on the Yalma River, a mission which the Indians were beginning to approach. Now they have run away and no one will be able to reach them. Guzman, who was attempting to bring fifty families to Brazil, has been arrested. But the wrong has been done and the Indians are becoming continually more savage and impossible to find.

Genocchi was particularly accurate in pointing out the responsibility of the authorities. At times the government arrested a rubber trader, an

---

[30] AGG. S.7/23.
[31] G. Genocchi to Filippo Tolli, February 2, 1912. AGG. L.18/T.

assassin or a trader of boys who was caught at the scene of his crime. He was then inevitably released for "lack of evidence."

> It is incredible with what indifference Indians are bought and sold in Iquitos, are stolen from nearby tribes by fraud and violence, often with the shedding of blood. Government employees very often turn this convenient custom to their own profit.

Consequently it was natural that several rubber traders and employees viewed missions among the Indians as smoke in their eyes. "A short time ago a Peruvian told Father L. Alvarez that the missionaries ought to be treated as criminals because, by instructing the Indians, they deprive us of our beasts of burden." Genocchi, who recorded the testimony of Father Alvarez, commented: "This man only translated in clear-cut language the ideas which are dominant in Peru's uncultivated regions. Unfortunately, many of the government's employees are of the same opinion, but they fear the press and England." According to Genocchi, "The government must grant greater security, and perhaps declare certain territories, alloted to the missions, to be inaccessible, like the ancient cities of refuge." [32]

---

[32] G. Genocchi to Cardinal R. Merry del Val, February 29, 1912. ASV.SS. F.4. 88.

CHAPTER VII

THE ECCLESIASTICAL SITUATION IN IQUITOS

Genocchi's delicate task of establishing a new mission for the Indians was equally as important as collecting information regarding their situation. This was actually the ultimate purpose of Genocchi's visit to Iquitos. To this difficult enterprise he had to devote great effort and extraordinary prudence. Before ever considering missions for the Indians, the most urgent matter to be addressed was the need for ecclesiastical reorganization at Iquitos itself. "I do not think that I shall have to modify the opinion which I have already formed," Genocchi wrote to Cardinal Merry del Val, "that is, that we must begin from Iquitos, which is the natural center of any mission one may establish for the poor Indians in the vast Peruvian territory, bordering with Ecuador, Colombia and Brazil." [1]

On his arrival at Iquitos Genocchi had found the city in a state of both civil and ecclesiastical anarchy. Genocchi described Iquitos as "one of the richest cities of Peru, from which the government draws wealth from the duty on rubber alone." [2] To give Cardinal Merry del Val an idea of the administrative anarchy, Genocchi called his attention to one fact. The City Hall did not establish a house of isolation for the sick until the yellow fever epidemic had run for several months. Hundreds of lives had already been lost to the epidemic and only a minimal number of the sick were treated in the isolation center when it was established. Fortunately, the rains were beginning to wash the streets. These were unpaved and the middle of the road was an open ditch where all of the garbage was thrown. Only on the main streets were there sidewalks. Yellow fever found an excellent terrain. "One readily understands," Genocchi commented, "the discontent of this population which so often threatens to break away from the mother country. The employees come here to get rich and the majority shrink neither from fraud nor from bribery nor from conniving with criminals." [3]

---

[1] G. Genocchi to Cardinal R. Merry del Val, January 2, 1912. ASV.SS. F. 4. 86.
[2] G. Genocchi to Cardinal R. Merry del Val, February 9, 1912. ASV.SS. F. 4. 86.
[3] G. Genocchi ro Cardinal R. Merry del Val, February 9, 1912. ASV.SS. F.4. 86.

The ecclesiastical situation was even worse. Iquitos was the see of the Prefecture Apostolic of San León de Amazonas, which was entrusted to the Augustinian Fathers. From the very creation of the Prefecture Apostolic, there was a dispute going on concerning the jurisdiction of the parish of Iquitos. According to the Presidential decree of October 27, 1898, there was no doubt that Iquitos belonged to the Prefecture Apostolic of San León de Amazonas. On March 6, 1907, Father Pedro Correa, the parish priest of Iquitos, had offered his submission to the Prefect Apostolic, Father Diaz. However, on April 13 of the same year the government had issued a decree stating that the parish of Iquitos belonged to the Diocese of Chachapoyas.

On February 4, 1910, Father Diaz sent a circular letter to the priests of the Prefecture claiming jurisdiction over Iquitos. Polemics ensued in the newspapers. The bishop of Chachapoyas intervened in support of the Prefect Apostolic of San León de Amazonas and sent the following statement to the newspaper *El Herald*. It was published November 11, 1910.

> Why call my letter in which I recognized the Apostolic Prefect's jurisdiction over Iquitos an unprecedented attempt? The division between the Prefecture Apostolic and my diocese is a territorial one, and the Prefecture's territory includes Iquitos. That this was accepted by the Peruvian government is evident from the following letter of Dr. Tel. Orihuela, Minister of Cult, to the Prefect of Loreto:
>
> "Lima, March 12, 1903.
>
> The borders of these Prefectures were established not on the basis of the population but on the basis of territory. Thus, if within a certain territory there are some civilized villages along with uncivilized tribes, the jurisdiction of the Prefecture Apostolic extends to one and the other, because it would not be possible to have a discontinuity in the area of the same Prefecture. The same person created the Prefecture, and established the territory which it controls." [4]

Genocchi informed Cardinal Merry del Val that "the Supreme Government's decision of April 13, 1907, with a stroke of the pen, cancelled the decree of the Sacred Congregation for the Propagation of the Faith, taking Iquitos and the other civilized centers away from the jurisdiction of the Prefect Apostolic, and claiming to subject them to the bishop of Chachapoyas." Father Correa had taken advantage of the government's decree to refuse to recognize the jurisdiction of the Prefect Apostolic. When Genocchi arrived in Iquitos and questioned

---

[4] AGG. S.7/21.

him, Father Correa openly declared his rejection of the jurisdiction of the Prefecture Apostolic. At the same time the Peruvian priest instigated the population against the Augustinians, who were foreigners. In his letter to Cardinal Merry del Val Genocchi continued as follows:

> Father Correa has affirmed to me that the jurisdiction of the Prefect Apostolic, according to the decision of the *Patrono* which is the Peruvian government, extends itself only to the missions among the Indians. Iquitos would still depend on the bishop of Chachapoyas. The latter has loyally declared more than once that he has nothing to do with Iquitos, but it does not matter. It is the *Patrono* who rules! Thus Father Correa, like the priest of Yurimayuas, an important city, and the other two or three priests who do as they like in the Apostolic Prefecture, does not depend on anyone, and does not care. Indeed as Peruvians they boast of the government's support, and seek to keep alive the population's hatred of the foreign invaders, the poor Augustinian missionaries, who are all Spaniards.

On the other hand, the new Prefect Apostolic, Father Prat who was "a man of great meekness, piety, and good will," did not have the strength to face this situation. He had only one young priest with him. Three or four others were in missionary stations. Genocchi continued in his letter:

> From the long letter which I wrote to the Apostolic Delegate in Peru, a lengthy passage from which I enclose here, your Eminence will understand the very difficult position of the Augustinian missionaries. I wrote of it also, although more briefly, to the Sacred Congregation for the Propagation of the Faith. By the same carrier I am sending an issue of a local newspaper *El Oriente* with an impressive article on the religious question in Iquitos, and with many other useful items (see p. 12). ... The situation of the Augustinians is unsustainable in Iquitos.

Nevertheless, Genocchi added that "a large part of the best families respect and esteem the Augustinians. Their school is well attended, as is their little private chapel." [5]

As for the diocesan priests in Iquitos, Genocchi informed the Secretary of State that the single parish of at least 15,000 people (about another 1,000 were Jews and foreigners who were Christians only insofar as they had been baptized) was run by Father Correa. The other two or three secular priests were "merchants, drinkers, and living in

---

[5] G. Genocchi to Cardinal R. Merry del Val, January 2, 1912. ASV.SS. F.4. 85, 81, 85.

concubinage."[6] It is a known fact that towards the end of the colonial period the clergy of Peru fell into a most degraded and demoralized condition, owing largely to the benefices given to Spanish priests. They accepted them as stepping stones for promotion to better positions in Spain or Mexico. As a result, the higher clergy took very little interest in their subordinates, who generally came from the lower class. Like any other branch of Spanish administrative circles, promotion was closed to the colonial born. The war of independence and a long series of revolutionary wars sustained this state of corruption in the Church. Bishops were chosen by the government which retained the right of nomination to a vacant see. In choosing, the government was guided more by the political pliability of the bishops than by any regard for their piety or religious zeal. The bishops' stipends were apt to fluctuate if they did not respond to the exigencies of the party in power.[7]

The so-called parochial church of Iquitos, Genocchi informed Cardinal Merry del Val and the Apostolic Delegate in Lima, was a kind of "low and narrow shed where the heat was unbearable." A good woman had told him with conviction that in the present situation there was no obligation to attend Mass in Iquitos. The government had provided land for a new church. On the surface of the ground there were the foundations for a suitable church. Already, 24,000 *soles* [600 pounds] had been spent on it. The *junta* of the department contributed 1,000 pounds yearly. The Prefect of Iquitos, to whom Genocchi introduced himself with a letter from the Minister of Cult in Lima, declared that with that sum of money nothing could be done.

> The best though is this. The *junta* has discovered that by continuing to construct the church upon the foundations already laid, the artistic standpoint of the square (which does not exist, there being nothing but a field and a few houses and cabins) would suffer. Thus twelve or fifteen feet will be eliminated from the front of the church, which may perhaps be extended in the rear. Consequently there are new studies, new projects and new illicit gains. To the great consolation of the ruling Masonry, the church will be put off until doomsday, and much money will flow into the pockets of the interested parties. I am trying hard to persuade the Catholics I meet to protest as a group and not to tolerate such iniquity. But here they are as accustomed to abuses of power as in Turquia, and Lima is far away.[8]

---

[6] G. Genocchi to Msgr. A. Scapardini, December 31, 1911. ASV.DP. F.4. 30.

[7] See Marcel Monnier, *Des Andes au Para* (Paris: chez Plon, 1890). The author describes the Peruvian and Ecuadorian clergy of the eighteenth century and the decadence of the missions.

[8] G. Genocchi to Msgr. A. Scapardini, December 31, 1911. ASV.DP. F.4. 30.

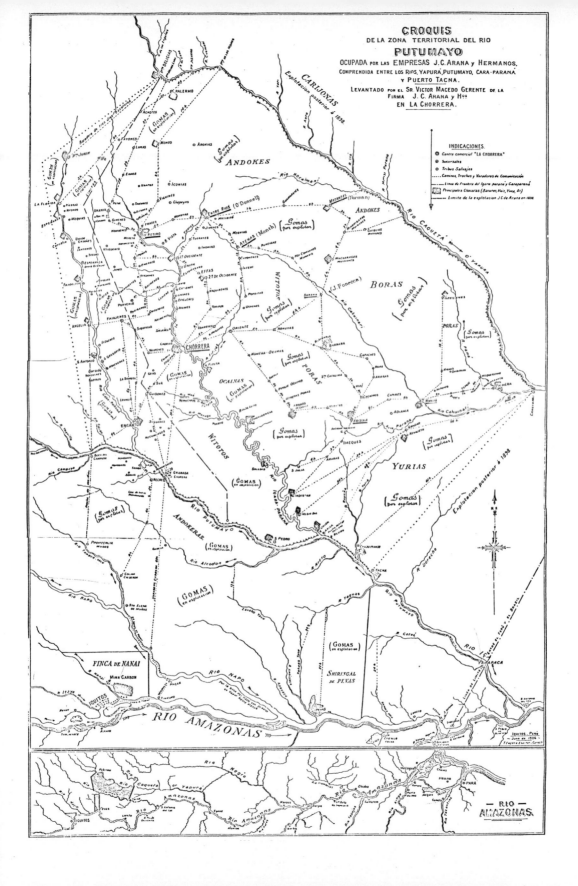

With these conditions the Catholics were terribly handicapped. Genocchi wrote that in all of Iquitos there were not one hundred persons who went to Mass on Sunday. "Decency was lost because of all the public concubinage and the embezzlement of the Indians." [9]

* * *

The solution for this state of affairs was to construct the church as soon as possible and to settle the question of the ecclesiastical situation in Iquitos. With this in mind Genocchi wrote to the Apostolic Delegate in Lima, suggesting that he deal with the government and persuade them to send by telegraph an absolute veto to change the plan of the church:

> You know that for the laying of the foundation-stone alone 200 pounds were wasted to quench the thirst and to fill the pocket of a few. Then there was a deficit and flight of the cashier. Then 24,000 *soles* [600 pounds] were spent on the foundation which now they would like not to use because the axis of the church is parallel to the side-street, and not perpendicular to the axis of the square. A certain Marazzini, an Italian disbeliever, being a town-councellor, proposed not to mar the plan of the church, and showed how one could provide aesthetics without touching the foundation. He asked also that instead of two towers, which were too expensive, only one be built. His fair proposals, which naturally diminished the profit of the engineers and of the others, were not accepted. So only the direct intervention of the government can put an end to this scandal. The body of the church could be built right away, and afterwards one could think about the façade and the ornaments. [10]

In addition, the Apostolic Delegate should try, if possible, to settle the question of ecclesiastical jurisdiction, at least provisionally, through a written declaration of the government. However, Genocchi realized that it would be difficult to obtain such a declaration and did not dare to hope for it. The real solution would be to erect Iquitos as the see of a bishop. "We shall not witness an effective arrangement," Genocchi stated, "until a Peruvian bishop has been established in Iquitos."

> The people want the bishop and so does the government, but first there must be a church and an episcopal house, possibly annexed to the church. I have noted that no one has thought about the house. [11]

---

[9] G. Genocchi to Msgr. A. Scapardini, December 31, 1911. ASV.DP. F.4. 30.
[10] G. Genocchi to Msgr. A. Scapardini, January 13, 1912. ASV. DP. F.4. 31, 32.
[11] G. Genocchi to Msgr. A. Scapardini, December 31, 1911. ASV.DP. F.4. 31.

The leader of Iquitos needed two qualifications: he had to be a bishop and he had to be a Peruvian. Genocchi wrote to Cardinal Merry del Val: "An intelligent, zealous and energetic leader, who can be no other than a Peruvian bishop, must reside there. If he is not a bishop he will not be heard by the government and the people. If he is not Peruvian worse still, although the missionaries under his jurisdiction can be of any nation. Greater details in time." [12]

Msgr. Quattrocchi, whom Genocchi considered to be the most intelligent, able and upright man that the Holy See could wish to have in that region, suggested the young bishop of Chachapoyas, Msgr. Lisson, for the position in Iquitos. Msgr. Quattrocchi often spoke in admiration of Msgr. Lisson and even the people of Iquitos held him in high esteem.

---

[12] G. Genocchi to Cardinal R. Merry del Val, January 2, 1912. ASV.SS. F.4, 86.

CHAPTER VIII

THE INDIANS OF BRAZIL
AND OF THE AMAZON BASIN

On January 28, 1912, Genocchi informed his friend Cardinal Capecelatro that his task in Iquitos was accomplished: "Yellow fever, which has killed several of my fellow travellers, has spared me thus far. By February 10, I shall be able to leave with a good steamship. In Belém do Pará I shall inform you whether I shall return at once to Italy or shall go somewhere else. The mosquitos, the heat and a little trembling due to the quinine I take every day do not permit me to write as I would like." [1]

On February 9, Genocchi notified Cardinal Merry del Val that he was about to leave Iquitos. After a brief stop in Manaus, he would reach Belém do Pará. There he would await orders from the Holy See. On February 11, he embarked on the *Huaiana* with Father Alemany who was on his way to Lima. In Manaus Genocchi was received by the Italian Capuchins. They had been entrusted with the evangelization of a great Brazilian Amazon territory bordering on Peru. This stop-over was necessary to afford Genocchi the possibility to look into the condition of the Indians in the vast Amazon basin and in Brazil in general. There he was able to formulate the final project for the mission to be established in the Putumayo.

Genocchi's first source of information on the condition of the Indians in the district of Río Negro was a book by Alfred R. Wallace, *A Narrative of Travel on the Amazon and Rio Negro*. Before treating the matter of the four Indian tribes in the area — the Uaupes, the Cobeus, the Tarianas, and the Tucanos — Genocchi records Wallace's comments on the Río Negro. Wallace had arrived at the city of Barra on the Río Negro in the evening after the sun had set on the yellow Amazon River. In the morning he was surprised to see a change in the water. It was black as ink everywhere except where the white sand, seen in shallow water just a few feet through its dusky wave, appeared with a golden hue. "The water itself [was] of a pale brown color, the tinge being just

---

[1] G. Genocchi to Cardinal A. Capecelatro, January 28, 1912. AGG. L.3/C.

perceptible in a glass, while in deep water it appear[ed] jet black, and well deserves its name of Río Negro — Black River." [2]

Genocchi gives a detailed description of the Uaupes tribesmen. Their hair was carefully parted in the middle, combed behind the ears, tied in a long tail reaching three feet down the back and firmly bound with a long cord of very soft monkey's hair. A comb of palm wood and grass was worn in the hair. It was decorated with feathers which gave a feminine appearance to the face, even more so because of the total absence of a beard. The women, on the other hand, wore their hair moderately long but without ornaments. They were absolutely naked. Genocchi then goes on to relate the initiation rites for the girls and boys. At the first sign of puberty, the girls undergo a trying ordeal. For the months preceding they are secluded in the house and allowed only a small quantity of bread and water. At the end of the month all the relatives and friends of the parents assemble, each of them bringing pieces of *sipo* [an elastic climber]. The girl is then led out. Each person present gives her five or six severe blows with *sipo* across the back and the breast until she falls unconscious or, as sometimes happens, dead. If she recovers, the ceremony is repeated four times at intervals of six hours and it is considered an offense to the parents not to strike hard. During this time a large variety of meat and fish is prepared. The *sipos* are dipped into the pots and given her to lick. She is then considered a woman and proclaimed marriageable. The boys undergo a somewhat similar ordeal as an initiation into manhood but it is less severe.

The dead were almost always buried in the houses. The Tarianas and Tucanos Indians disinterred the decomposed corpse about a month after the death. It was placed in a large pan or kettle over a fire, until all the volatile parts were driven off with a horrible odor, leaving only a black carbonaceous mass. This was pounded into a fine powder and mixed in several large vats of caxiri. It was drunk by the assembled company until all was consumed. They believed that with this ceremony the virtues of the deceased were transmitted to them. Among the four tribes the Cobeus Indians were the only cannibals. Genocchi provides some dreadful details. The Cobeus Indians ate members of other tribes killed in battle and even made war for the express purpose of procuring human flesh for food. When they had more than they could consume at once, they smoked the flesh over the fire and preserved it a long time for food.

---

[2] Alfred R. Wallace, *A Narrative of Travels on the Amazon and Rio Negro with an Account of the Native Tribes* (New York: Greenwood Press, 1892)., p. 112.

Concerning the beliefs of these Indians, Genocchi found they were at the same stage as those of the natives of New Guinea. The Indians did not have any belief that could really be classified as a religion. They appeared to have no definite idea of God. They had a much more definite idea of a bad spirit, "jurupari", or devil, whom they feared. When it thundered, they said that the "jurupari" was angry, and their idea of natural death was that the "jurupari" killed them. They had numerous *pagés*, a kind of priest similar to the "medicine-men" of the North American Indians. These were believed to have great power to propitiate the bad spirit, to be able to cure all diseases by charms and to destroy enemies.

Genocchi also tells of some deeds of the white men living in the same district which Wallace had recorded in his book. A Brazilian from Pernanbuco was banished to Río Negro for taking part in an insurrection. Residing in Wanawaca, he had murdèred the Indians, carried away their wives and daughters and committed barbarities that were too disgusting to mention. He received Wallace with great civility, gave him a very good breakfast and conversed "in an unusually rational manner." Later, *Señor* L. [sic] asked Wallace if he were not surprised to see such a mild-looking man. "But these soft-spoken ones are always the worst," *Señor* L. said. "He is a regular hypocrite, and he will stop at nothing. To his friends he boasts of his crimes and declares that there is nothing that he will not do for his own pleasure or profit." Another day Wallace was introduced to L.'s family which consisted of two young and two grown-up daughters and a little boy of eight years. A good-looking *mameluca* of about thirty was introduced as the mother of his young children. L. informed Wallace that he did not believe in marriage and thought anyone who did was a great fool. He pointed out the advantages of keeping oneself free of such ties by saying that he turned out the mother of his two elder daughters because she had grown old, and he got a younger woman in her place.

The merchants and authorities in Barra and Pará would ask the traders among the Indians to procure a boy or girl for them, well aware of the only manner in which they could be obtained. In fact, the government "in some degree authorized the practice." L. had been "requested by two parties at Barra (one was the *Delegato de Policía*) to furnish them with an Indian girl." In Guia there was a man named Manoel Joaquím. It was believed that he had murdered his wife and because of this crime and others had been banished to Rio Negro. There he used to threaten the Indians, shoot at them and take their daughters and wives from them. The people of Guia said Joaquim had murdered two Indian girls and committed many other horrible crimes.

At this point Genocchi records a conversation between Wallace and a certain Frei José. The conversation was about the existence of smallpox in Pará. Frei José related an "anecdote of his own diplomatic powers, with respect to that dreadful disease, on which powers he appeared to pride himself considerably." When he was a soldier in Bolivia there were several tribes of very warlike Indians who plundered and murdered travellers on the way to Santa Cruz. The President sent the soldiers after them and spent much money on gunpowder and bullets but with very little effect. Smallpox spread through the city and the clothes of all who died of it were ordered to be burned to prevent infection. One day, while conversing with the President about the Indians, Frei suggested a much cheaper way to exterminate them than using gunpowder and bullets. "Instead of burning the clothes," he said, "just order them to be put in the path of the Indians. They are sure to take them, and they will die off like wildfire." The President followed this advice and, in a few months, no more was heard of plundering by the Indians. Four or five tribes were thus totally exterminated.[3]

Genocchi's other source of information about the Río Negro district was the pastoral letter of the bishop of Manaus, Msgr. Frederick Costa. In this letter dated April 11, 1909, the bishop quoted Germano Garrito, his host on his visit to the Río Negro. He wrote: "Negro slavery came to an end in May, 1888, but today a more barbaric slavery exists than that of the Negroes, the slavery of our Indians. What goes on in our environs is incredible." The bishop added:

> Today we can and must say that Germano's statement is pure truth. It makes our heart bleed to say it, but there still are slaves in Brazil and they are our Indians. ... Some merchants arrive in a village with carbine in hand. They do not ask questions, they demand. And often they take and violate Indian girls. With a small portion of spirits they attract the incautious, men and women, and they do such things which the pen refuses to describe. They seize them by force, they tie them to the bottom of a canoe and whip them so barbarously that we can find examples only in the history of Roman Slavery. What shall we say then of the raids in the forest to find an Indian fleeing from slavery? They capture those of his village. And how do they treat the fugitive if he falls into the hands of his master? We will not say. ... And the greatest cause for shame is that **many times the authorities are conniving** ..., and not only conniving, but also **protecting, organizing, and carrying out such raids**" [Genocchi's emphasis].[4]

* * *

---

[3] AGG. S.7/22. See A. R. Wallace, *Op. Cit.*, p. 345, 346, 139, 143-144, 207, 224-225.

[4] G. Genocchi to Cardinal R. Merry del Val, March, 29, 1912. ASV.SS. F.4. 104.

As for the ecclesiastical situation, the clergy left much to be desired. "The clergy are few in number," Genocchi informed the Secretary of State, "and collected at random." There was no seminary. Even the secondary school, run by ecclesiastics, which could afford hope for some vocations, no longer existed. From Wallace's book, Genocchi recorded the following fact: The same Frei José who had suggested to the President of Bolivia the cheapest way to eliminate the Indians, had become a friar in a convent and later a parish priest. He told tales of his convent life which Genocchi compared to the tales of Chaucer. Wallace heard these tales and commented, "Don Juan was innocent compared with Father Frei José." But José told him, "I have a great respect for my cloth and I never do anything disreputable — **during the day!**" [Genocchi's emphasis].[5]

The Capuchins of Manaus were just beginning their mission. They had only two priests and one layman in Sao Paolo d'Olivenza where they were building a church and residence themselves and even making their own bricks. Two laymen and the other four priests (including the Prefect Apostolic) attended to the church of Sao Sebastiao and to religious institutions in Manaus. They would receive reinforcements from Italy, but they could do little or nothing until the house at Olivenza and at least another shelter in their Prefecture were completed. They had already crossed part of the territory and many died from the unbearable climate and excessive workload. The group was in great need of material means and had to pay 500 Italian lire for the rent of the house at Manaus belonging to the bishopric. The bishop hoped to be able to free them of that heavy burden, but there was reason to fear that the good man's hope would come to nothing. Genocchi concluded: "It is voiced that the Capuchins would have to pay 1,000 Italian lire monthly in rent instead of the 500 which they now pay, on the demand of an administration in which the bishop seems to have little say. If this threat were to come true, they would probably have to give up Manaus and the Prefecture."[6]

North of Manaus was the Vicariate Apostolic of Río Branco entrusted to the Benedictine Abbot, Msgr. Van Caloen. With the information obtained from eyewitnesses, Genocchi could inform the Congregation of Religious that Msgr. Van Caloen, "very commendable for what he had done at the beginning, became intolerable to his confreres and to others." They called him "despotic, arbitrary, and

[5] AGG. S.7/22. See A. R. Wallace, *Op. Cit.*, p. 157.
[6] G. Genocchi to Cardinal R. Merry del Val, March 1st, 1912. ASV.SS. F.4. 102.

ostentatious, a man who takes care of his poor health with the luxury and services of a gentleman."

He had himself named Vicar Apostolic of Río Branco because of his mania for becoming bishop. It is certain that he never went to Río Branco and it is easy to foresee that he never will go. At the most he would travel as long as he could have comforts. And that poor mission languishes, although one must also admit that it is in a very difficult territory. I believe that Msgr. Van Caloen is an exhausted man who has given all he had (and it was not a little) and cannot give any more good to the Church of Brazil.

Further, Genocchi said that he heard how the wealth of the Benedictines was a cause of scandal and danger. He learned this from many travellers after discussing religious conditions in Brazil with them. Genocchi was convinced that the government would take by force the national wealth which the Benedictines exploited. They did the country some good with a school in Rio de Janeiro, an improved marshland on some estate, etc., but all this was very little in comparison with the incoming revenue, Genocchi related. He felt that the Benedictines should part with the greater portion of the real estate, and invest the money in some great works of charity. "The money could be used for Christian education, preferably for houses of refuge for the poor workers, for old people, for abandoned children and for missions, with respective institutions for Blacks and Indians." Genocchi wrote: "The envy which the wealth of the Benedictines excites flows in part onto other religious congregations, which suffer on the occasion of revolts or of an unfavorable legislature. If the wealth of the religious is nearly always the cause of corruption, the ostentation of the wealth is certainly the cause, more or less remote, of confiscation and suppressions, especially in our time." [7]

* * *

In addition to the detailed information about the districts of Río Negro and Río Branco, Genocchi's last report to the Holy See informed Cardinal Merry del Val of the condition of the Indians in Brazil. With few exceptions, the same crimes committed in Peru and the neighboring republics were committed in Brazil. Two conditions contributing to the spread of these crimes were almost the same everywhere. These conditions were, first, the perversity of the irreligious and degenerate rubber traders, and, second, the remoteness of any control on them by

---

[7] G. Genocchi to Cardinal G. Gotti, March 30, 1913. ACPF. R.151. 639.

the government. It was appropriate to say *ab uno disce omnes* [if you know one you know them all]: "I refrain from mentioning what Mr. Casement, the Consul General, wrote in his reports, with which your Eminence is already well acquainted. Here I shall simply note several facts and documents in my possession which cannot at all be denied and are not found in Casement's reports." [8]

The documents consisted of two publications addressed to a national audience. The Brazilians Olavo Bilac and M. Bonfim had published a reader entitled *Atravez do Brazil* for the intermediate course of primary schools. As its object, Genocchi said, the authors proposed: "to give young people a **current** [Genocchi's emphasis] and concrete view of Brazilian life, with candor, even when this view offers facts or events which **perhaps (?)** [Genocchi's comment] seem cruel." [9] In chapter thirty-seven they described how the inland local important people had real torture rooms in their own homes, complete with the well-known stocks and other instruments of torture. This existed even in areas not far from the coast. A poor boy mistakenly taken for a thief was whipped and placed with his left foot and right hand in the shackles and left in that terrible position a whole night. Later on, that same boy almost died in the shackles from blows of a lacerating whip. In reality he was an innocent foreigner.[10]

In the *Revista do Muzeo Paulista* in Brazil, Dr. H. Jhering, the director, wrote that "the best thing would be to exterminate the Indians." [11] In the same review there was a protest which, however, stated: "Jhering is trying to sanction a cruelty **which has been committed against the natives for a long time** [Genocchi's emphasis]. ... The present generation is responsible for it on account of the lack of legislation." Genocchi added:

> It could thus continue to cite indisputable documents and witnesses if what occurs in Brazil and in the other republics had not already been manifested. The Brazilians say (and more than one person has said it to me as well) that the Peruvians are a good deal more cruel, and that while the Brazilians kill and chastise for utilitarian ends, the Peruvians often massacre and torture for sheer pleasure. I think that, necessary exceptions being made, this is true.[12]

---

[8] G. Genocchi to Cardinal R. Merry del Val, March 29, 1912. ASV.SS. F.4. 101.
[9] Olavo Bilac & M. Bonfin, *Atravez do Brasil* (Rio de Janeiro: Alves, 1910), p. viii.
[10] *Ibid.* p. 150f.
[11] AGG. S.7/24. See *Revista do Muzeo Paulista*, 7 (1908), p. 215.
[12] G. Genocchi to Cardinal R. Merry del Val, March 29, 1912. ASV.SS. F.4. 102.

After that Genocchi related two testimonies which he gathered during his long journey from Belém do Pará to Iquitos. Manuel Leite, a mulatto of about eighteen and his brother, José, a pure blood of fifteen, attended secondary school in Oporto and traveled with Genocchi from Belém do Pará to Leiroes. They were sons of a rich rubber trader of the Acre, the Brazilian province bordering on Peru and Bolivia. Genocchi soon made friends with them and asked them to recount what interested him. They said that "all the owners and rubber traders have shackles and whips." According to the two boys, often the shackles were not merely for two feet. There were others for the hands alone or for the hands and neck. These were so placed that the body was strained and the victim could not move a limb. For slight misdeeds the victim remained in the shackles for a couple of days. For more serious ones, for as long as a month and more. In the shackles, they received daily a little bread and water and considerable blows with a rod. The master was the ultimate judge and had torturers at his command. If on a rare occasion a government employee was within seeing distance, he looked the other way and allowed the master to do what he wanted. Sometimes the government employees themselves were active accomplices of those who corrupted them by offering bribes of money or even gifts of male and female slaves.

The famous English explorer, Henry Savage Landor, was making a journey on foot across Brazil. He spent ten days with Genocchi en route between Manaus and Iquitos. He reported that "there was real slavery of the Indians everywhere." Genocchi, who related this conversation in his report, added that Landor stated: "The Indians had been reduced to such a small number that, according to his opinion, the whole population of Brazil of all colors probably did not exceed seven or eight million, and that official statistics were exaggerated out of vanity." [13] In a letter to his Jewish friend, Levi della Vida, Genocchi revealed a detail which showed how widespread the practice of slavery had become. After agreeing that the Christian religion does not reconcile itself with slavery or any other form of violence, Genocchi added that "in Brazil [he] knew that Franciscans, Jesuits, and Mercederians (these last instituted for the redemption of slaves) had slaves, naturally under slave regulation, until 1888, when slavery ceased to be legal." [14]

The documentation provided by Genocchi concerning slavery clearly shows the role that sensuality played in the most cruel form of

[13] G. Genocchi to Cardinal R. Merry del Val, March 29, 1912. ASV.SS. F.4. 102.
[14] G. Genocchi to Giorgio Levi della Vida, November 20, 1915. AGG. L.10/L.

slavery and in the sadism of which the slaves were often victims. He thus ends his report:

> It really seems as if the white people in equatorial countries hold the ancient expression *Ultra aequinoctialem non peccavi* [beyond the equinox I did not sin] to be true. All is permitted there and nothing is sinful. Unfortunately, young people are especially taught that sexual intercourse, whatever the Friars may say, is always good and that it pleases God who said: *Crescite et multiplicamini* [be fruitful and multiply. Gen. 1:28]. I have heard this sacrilegious teaching several times with my own ears. For this purpose everyone wants little Indian slave girls, who are forced to submit to the most shameless and insatiable will. It is true today what Father Manoel de Nobrega said at that time in his famous letter to the king (in the year 1549): "The inland regions of the country are filled with sons of Christians who multiply according to pagan customs." In Iquitos there is a man who had more than sixty children from no one knows how many women. And there are those who envy him and propose him as a model.[15]

After ten days in Manaus, Genocchi left for Belém do Pará on February 24. During his journey down the Amazon River he had an interesting conversation with a man named Montenegrin, who was born in Brazil of a Neapolitan father and who lived long among the rubber traders. Genocchi also spoke with an old Portuguese who had been in those parts for over forty years. One of these declared, among other things, that it was impossible to gain very much without barbarities.

* * *

On reaching Belém do Pará, Genocchi managed to communicate the plan for the mission for the Indians to Cardinal Merry del Val. Further information gathered during his journey from Iquitos led him to modify his opinion regarding the headquarters of the missionaries. The greatest difficulty lay in the unhealthiness of the territory. A large part of the Peruvian soldiers sent to the Putumayo and to the Coquetá perished there after a few months or returned in pitiable condition. Genocchi knew that there would be rubber traders on the boat he was to take from Iquitos. They had a long experience of these inhospitable territories. By questioning the traders, Genocchi could supplement the information he had already gathered in Iquitos. After doing so, Genocchi no longer had any doubt that the best place for a mission was

---

[15] G. Genocchi to Cardinal R. Merry del Val. March 29, 1921. ASV.SS. F.4. 104.

not at Iquitos but at La Chorrera. It was located on the Igaraparaná, a
small tributary of the Putumayo.

> There one would have high ground, and a cascade for fresh and healthy
> water; whilst the distance from Iquitos is only that of an eight or ten
> days journey. Also there are frequent communications by steamboats on
> the Putumayo and the Napo Rivers (the mouths of which are quite near
> Iquitos), the journey being neither long nor difficult. Three or four
> missionaries should reside at La Chorrera, and from there visit the
> nearby Indian tribes whose members are still in great part the victims of
> the infamous Arana Company.

Genocchi ended his report by remarking that the perpetrators of
the more enormous crimes were either in prison at Iquitos (it was
feared, however, that they would never be judged) or escaped beyond
the boundaries. Nevertheless there would always be rubber traders
seeing profit in those prolific forests.[16]

In Belém do Pará Genocchi had to face the problem of continuing
his trip to Colombia, according to the instructions received from the
Secretary of State. After an exchange of telegrams between Genocchi
and Cardinal Merry del Val, and between the latter and the Apostolic
Delegate in Bolivia, it was decided to leave the decision to Genocchi. It
seemed to him that there was little advantage in his going to Colombia.
It was useless to consider going to Venezuela, not to mention Ecuador.
Moreover, one month would not be enough to reach Colombia from
Belém do Pará, given the infrequent connections of the steamship. On
the other hand, the journey from Europe to Colombia lasted ten or
twelve days. Acting upon the conviction that he had already good and
sufficient information about South America, and given the urgency of
the project for the Putumayo, Genocchi decided that it was better to
return directly to Rome. On March 7, Genocchi informed the Secretary
of State about his decision and the details of his itinerary. Because there
were no steamships from Belém do Pará to Italy, Genocchi would leave
the following day aboard an English steamship which went directly to
Lisbon, then Vigo. He would not disembark at Lisbon because several
Portuguese Jesuits had dissuaded him by their insistence on the danger
of doing so. From Vigo, Genocchi would go by railroad to Barcelona,
where he intended to spend a few days at the house of his confreres. He
would then proceed immediately to Italy. In the same letter, Genocchi
assured Cardinal Merry del Val that he had already sent the plan
concerning the Putumayo mission.

---

[16] G. Genocchi to Cardinal R. Merry del Val, February 29, 1912. ASV.SS. F.4. 89.

I shall be able to give further details in person, having sought during my journey to inquire into everything from every sort of person, so that I think I shall be able to answer any questions which your Eminence will perhaps need to ask me and which are difficult to foresee from here. I am leaving with many written notes and newspapers in different languages, especially English, Spanish and Portuguese, for what I could find in them which would be useful in connection with the problem of the Indians. I had already stated in my first telegram that I was disposed to continue if the Holy See wished, since I still enjoy good health, but all things considered, it seems to me that it would be more useful if I return to Rome.[17]

Genocchi's arrival at Vigo was rather dramatic. A severe storm prevented the boat from coming alongside the warf and he agreed to being swung ashore on a rope. Genocchi reached the shore but the going was so rough that he broke several teeth. From Vigo, Genocchi reached Barcelona and in the quiet of his confreres' house, he completed his last report on South America on March 29. On March 31 he left Barcelona for Rome.

---

[17] G. Genocchi to Cardinal R. Merry del Val, March 7, 1912. ASV.SS. F.4. 104.

CHAPTER IX

THE ENGLISH MISSIONARIES

Father Genocchi arrived in Rome on April 4, 1912. On April 26, he met with Pope Pius X. The audience lasted a good while. The Holy Father's welcome to Father Genocchi must have been singularly hearty, considering his expectations and the zeal with which Father Genocchi had accomplished his mission. There is no record of the conversation between the Pope and the Apostolic Visitor. A letter of Genocchi to Cardinal Capecelatro contains the following modest allusion to the meeting:

> Last Friday I saw the Holy Father and stayed with him a long time. He demonstrated an extraordinary goodness, enough to exceed even the great kindness shown me at other times. He thanked me repeatedly for the little I had done in America, which to him appeared to be a great deal.[1]

The task which now lay before Genocchi was to assist the Secretary of State in three aspects of the new mission — first, in the ecclesiastical reorganization of Iquitos; then in the actual creation of a mission; and finally, in preparing the first group of missionaries. The Holy See could do nothing else but commend, support and adopt the proposal recommended in Genocchi's report No. 9.[2]

On April 23, 1912, Cardinal Merry del Val informed Msgr. Scapardini, Apostolic Delegate in Lima, of the conclusions reached with Genocchi. The report Genocchi had given him on the conditions of Iquitos both orally and in writing confirmed the information which had already reached the Holy See in this regard. This made it all the more evident that it was necessary to settle the ecclesiastical situation in the most convenient and effective way for that important city. As Genocchi noted, Iquitos was the natural center of all the missions already established or those about to be established for the benefit of the Indians who were scattered in those territories. Cardinal Merry del Val called attention to two aspects of the problem.

---

[1] G. Genocchi to Cardinal A. Capecelatro, May 3, 1912. AGG. L.3/C.
[2] See p. 95-96.

First, in reference to Genocchi's letter of December 31, 1911, and also to the instruction given to the Apostolic Delegate, the Secretary of State urged the Apostolic Delegate to inform the Holy See "whether and with what result he had thus far been able to do anything or hoped to do anything in the near future, so that with the approval and cooperation of the civil authorities a new diocese could be established there by the Holy See." It was planned that the diocese should have its see in Iquitos and that its bishop should be Peruvian. Both were considered of utmost importance by Genocchi; the former to promote a needed and salutary awakening of Christian life in Iquitos and the latter to make it possible for the missionaries to work more advantageously for the Indians. By the same token, Cardinal Merry del Val wished to know if the Apostolic Delegate had been able to obtain from the Peruvian government what Genocchi had recommended, i.e., the construction of the new church and a suitable residence near the church. This might accomodate the bishop and serve as the center of the mission for the Indians at the same time.

Second, concerning the establishment of the mission for the Indians, Cardinal Merry del Val informed the Apostolic Delegate that the Holy See had begun to take steps with the Father General of the Franciscans toward the establishment of a mission. The mission would be entrusted to the Irish Franciscans and would be located in La Chorrera on the Igaraparaná. This location, eight or ten days' distance from Iquitos, was suggested by Genocchi as a suitable residence for the missionaries because of the healthy climate and regular communication with the Putumayo and Napo. The missionaries would devote themselves to visiting the Indian tribes in the surrounding area who had been and continued to be oppressed and decimated by the Arana Company until that moment. Furthermore, the English nationality of the missionaries, given the respect and fear which England enjoyed there, would be helpful in repressing or restraining the cruelties against those poor natives.[3]

Before the proposal could be realized and put into effect, the intricate question concerning ecclesiastical jurisdiction over Iquitos and the adjacent territories, heretofore administered by a simple Prefect Apostolic, had to be settled. This was to involve months of laborious dealings with the Peruvian government. In fact it was only in the following autumn that the way was clear. The decree of the Congregation for the Propagation of the Faith, by which Pius X erected the mission of Putumayo, was signed October 4, 1912. The mission was

---

[3] Cardinal R. Merry del Val to Msgr. A. Scapardini, April 23, 1912. ASV.DP. F.4. 230.

taken from the Apostolic Prefecture of San León de Amazonas and included the territory from the left bank of the Aguarico, Napo and Amazon Rivers to the point where the Amazon enters Brazil.[4]

* * *

At the same time the Pope was at work drafting an encyclical condemning the atrocities committed against the Indians and pointing out ways to end the abuses by the rubber traders. Among Genocchi's papers there is a historical outline of pontifical documents concerning slavery, the abolition of slavery in modern times and a comment on the relationship between slavery and Christianity. It is a draft written in telegraphic style. Part is in Latin, part in French, part in English and part in German, evidently according to the sources which are not always given.

Nicolas V (1447-1455), in 1452 and in 1454 granted to the King of Portugal newly found lands and permission to sell the inhabitants into slavery.

Alexander VI (1492-1503), in the Bull *Inter caetera* of May 4, 1493, granted almost the same to Spain: land, islands etc., not people explicitly: "By the authority of Almighty God conferred upon us in Blessed Peter

---

[4] The decree, dated October 4, 1912, was published in *Acta Apostolicae Sedis* only on July 7, 1913. This is the text:

Apostolico zelo et paterna charitate curam suscipiens providendi lacrimabili conditioni Indorum latissimas regiones Americae Meridionalis incolentium, Ssmus Dñus noster Pius div. providentia PP. X, in suis encyclicis Literis sub die 7 iunii 1912, inter alia, propositum manifestavit novas disponendi missionales stationes, in quibus Indi ipsi perfugium et praesidium salutis invenirent. Nunc vero providum saluberrimumque consilium exsequi incipiens, erigendam statuit atque decrevit novam Missionem *de Putumayo* nuncupandam, cuius praecipua statio sit in loco *La Chorrera* dicto, quaeque regimini, administrationi et ecclesiastico ministerio missionariorum ex Ordine Fratrum Minorum Unionis Leonianae committatur ad nutum Sanctae Sedis.

De mandato igitur Sanctitatis Suae haec S. Congregatio christiano nomini propagando praeposita, Missionem, ut supra, *de Putumayo* denominandam per praesens Decretum erigit, eique tribuit et adsignat territorium quod per hoc idem Decretum dismembratur a latissima regione hactenus spectante ad praefecturam apostolicam S. Leonis de Amazonibus, spatium videlicet quod extenditur ab ora sinistra fluminum Aguarico, Napo et Amazonum usque ad punctum in quo flumen Amazonum attingit territorium brasiliense; septentrionem versus regionem Chorrera cum adiacentibus territoriis, reservata, ea ex parte, limitum descriptione ulterius pro rerum adiunctis determinanda.

Datum Romae ex aedibus S. Congregationis de Propaganda Fide, die 4 octobris 1912.

Fr. H. M. CARD. GOTTI, *Praefectus.*
C. Laurenti, *Secretarius.*

and of the vicarship of Jesus Christ, which we hold on earth, we, by tenor of these presents, should any of said islands have been found by your envoys and captains, do give, grant, and assign to you and your heirs and successors, kings of Castile and León forever with all their dominions, cities, camps, places and villages."

Pius II (1458-1464) on October 7, 1462 to the Bishop of Ruvo against negro slavery which he described as a "great crime." He animadverted the Bishop severely against those Christians who dragged neophytes into slavery.

Paul III (1534-1549), corrected his two predecessors [Nicolas V and Alexander VI] in this matter. Against the slavery of Indians. Approval of Jesuits (Their missions among the Indians). Peter Claver, S.J. (1580-1654).
In his Brief *Pastorale Officium* of May 29, 1537, to the Archbishop of Toledo, he excommunicated those who enslaved the Indians of America and confiscated their property.

Pius V (1566-1572) and Clement VIII (1592-1605), the same.

Urban VIII (1623-1644), in his letter of April 22, 1639, to the Collector of the Rights of the Apostolic Chamber in Portugal, excommunicated those who deal in slavery or keep Indians as slaves: "Who should dare or presume to reduce to slavery the western or southern Indians, to sell, to buy, to exchange, or to give them away, to separate them from their wives and children, or deprive them of their property and goods, to conduct or send them to other places, or in any manner to deprive them of liberty or retain them in slavery. ...."

Benedict XIV (1740-1758), in his letter of December 20, 1741, to the Bishops of Brazil and of certain other regions, reaffirmed the excommunication policy.

Pius VII (1800-1823), through his Secretary of State, Cardinal Ercole Consalvi, in the treaty of Vienna (1815) interposes his good offices with the leading heads of states to end negro slavery among Christians.

Gregory XVI (1831-1646), in his encyclical *In Supremo Apostolorum fastigio*, condemned all forms of colonial slavery and the slave trade, calling it *inhumanum illud commercium* [that inhuman trade].

Pius IX (1846-1878), in the Bull for the canonization of Peter Claver called slavery *summum nefas* [utmost abomination].

Leo XIII (1878-1903), in his encyclical *In plurimis* of May 5, 1888, stated: *Ad manumissionem libertatemque servorum noluit properare [Ecclesia], quod nisi tumultuose et cum suo ipsorum damno reipublicae detrimento fieri profecto non poterat* [The Church did not want to hasten the emancipation and freedom of slaves which could not be done without turbulence and harm to the nation].

The list of pontifical documents is followed by historical data concerning the abolition of slavery:

> The slavery of whites in Africa raised the first opposition of Christian Europe. Philip the Fearless conquered Tunisia. In 1389 an English expedition made the Arabs free their Christian slaves.

> George Fox and William Penn, founders of the Quakers, began the work. In 1751 the Quakers abolished slavery among them.

> On May 12, 1789, William Wilberforce, who won over the Ministers William Pitt and Charles J. Fox, asked (for the first time) for the abolition of slave trade in the English Parliament. He obtained it on February 23, 1808. On that day he exclaimed: "Never surely had I more cause for gratitude than now, when carrying the great object of my life, to which a gracious Providence directed my thoughts twenty-six or twenty-seven years ago and led my endeavours in 1787 or 1788."

> The decree [of the abolition of slave trade] received the royal signature on March 25 of the same year. From 1815 onward England made it a condition in treaties with all the nations.

> In 1833 Thomas F. Buxton, worthy emulator of Wilberforce (faithful right to the end), supported by the Christian movement (especially English women) obtained the suppression of slavery in the Colonies. England paid 20,000,000 pounds to emancipate her slaves.

> In 1848 the French Republic did likewise.

> In 1860 Abraham Lincoln was elected President. Civil war. In January 1, 1863 the decree of emancipation was published in Washington. In 1865, after the war, the emancipation was proclaimed and accepted by the whole United States.

Genocchi then cites without comment a statement by Ernest Renan: "*La papauté qui condamne si facilement et si imprudemment tant de choses, n'a pu encore se résoudre à condamner l'esclavage* [The papacy, which so easily and so imprudently condemns so many things, has not yet been able to made up its mind to condemn slavery]." Finally he explains in what sense Christianity is against slavery. François-Pierre Guillaume Guizot made the following statement:

> It has been often repeated that the abolition of slavery in the modern world was entirely due to Christianity. I believe that this is saying too much. Slavery existed for a long time in the bosom of Christianity without exciting astonishment or much opposition.

Genocchi answers by quoting the response of James Balmes taken from his book, *European Civilization.*

Christianity would have done wrong in trying to abolish slavery immediately. The spirit which animated the Church could not allow her rashly to enter on an enterprise which, without gaining the desired object, might have convulsed the world. The number of slaves was immense. Slavery was deeply rooted in laws, manners, ideas, and interest, individual and social. ... But Christianity has made a preparation for the abolition of slavery, when it stated: 'In Christ Jesus you are all sons of God. For as many of you as were baptized into Christ have put on Christ. There is neither Jew nor Greek, there is neither slave nor free, there is neither male nor female; for you are all one in Christ Jesus.' (Gal. 3:26-28. See also Col. 3:11).[5]

Genocchi comments: "In this way Christianity undermined the pagan concept of *slave-thing*. As soon as social and economic conditions permitted, slavery would fall apart and disappear, as in fact did happen little by little, by gradual and spontaneous disintegration." This was done through the Church as such, not through individuals. Genocchi turns to Balmes again:

It is by no means necessary that the merit of that conduct was understood by those who took part in it. It is not even necessary to suppose that the first Christians understood all the force of the tendencies of Christianity with respect to the abolition of slavery. What must be shown is that the result has been obtained by the doctrine and conduct of the Church.[6]

Genocchi adds: "It is *only* Christianity that has given man the sentiment of universal fraternity, that has made him lose the idea of *slave-thing*, and hence made slavery almost useless and fundamentally obnoxious to him."[7]

It may be asked whether Genocchi did this research for the purpose of drafting the pontifical document concerning slavery or for his own personal study. It is not possible to establish the reason.[8] Nevertheless, Genocchi proved that he was well informed on the encyclical that the Pope was preparing. At the end of May, he was able to apprise Cardinal Capecelatro that Pius X's first official action for the Indians had been accomplished. "The Pope's letter to the Bishops of

---

[5] J. Balmes, *European Civilization* (New York: J. Murphy Company, 1850), p. 91, 97.
[6] J. Balmes, *Op. Cit.*, p. 95.
[7] Ms. "Notes on Slavery". AGG. S.5/11.
[8] From consulting ASV (*Epistulae ad Principes, Positiones et Minutes*, N. 159, f. 55), I have found that the drafts of the Encyclical are not from the pen of Fr. Genocchi. I was unable to identify the author of the writing.

South America about the remedies to adopt against slavery and the destruction of the Indians is already written. For good considerations it will not be published until it has reached its destinations." [9]

* * *

Having finished his work at the Secretariate of State, Genocchi left for England on June 8, with the mandate "to deal with the question of establishing a mission in the Putumayo." [10] He had already notified the Apostolic Delegate at Lima on May 26, of his approaching trip to England and stated the reason for recruiting English missionaries: "According to my opinion what is important is that the missionaries be British subjects." They would establish the mission between the Napo River and the Putumayo River, and from there they will go to help the Indians. "Because of their presence alone, the Indians will be respected by the rubber traders." [11] Writing to Cardinal Capecelatro, Genocchi expressed some optimism. "The serious business for which I was sent to America and now to England seems to be proceeding well." There were certain points, he added, which required prudence, especially in dealing with the English government. The reasons were both political and religious. [12]

In its Memorandum to the Holy See the English government had presented the establishment of a Catholic mission in the Putumayo as "a personal opinion of the consular officer sent to Putumayo." Consequently the English government could not officially support the Catholic mission. Casement had shown his reports to the Anglican Archbishop of Canterbury, Randal Davidson. After perusing them the Archbishop wrote to Casement: "It is one of the blackest stories of cruelty that I have ever read." However, he expressed reticence and hesitancy concerning support for a Catholic mission. The following questions occurred to him: Does the mission have to be Catholic? Can the head of the Anglican Church support a Catholic mission? On March 13, 1912, after nine months of silence, Casement wrote of his disappointment to the Archbishop:

> I have lived so much abroad, and so much among savages, that I fear I have come to regard white men as a whole as Christians as a whole, and not sufficiently to realize the distinctions that exist at home, and separate them into separate schools of thought. In what I felt to be an appeal to a

---

[9] G. Genocchi to Cardinal A. Capecelatro, May 30, 1912. AGG. L.3/C.
[10] Cardinal R. Merry del Val to Msgr. M. Bidwell, June 6, 1912. ASV.SS. F.4. 111.
[11] G. Genocchi to Msgr. A. Scapardini, May 26, 1912. ASV.DP. F.4. 38.
[12] G. Genocchi to Cardinal A. Capecelatro, June 16, 1912. AGG. L.3/C.

common pity, and a common compassion that animated all kindly
civilized men, I was, I fear, underrating the influences that separate
Christian Churches, and perhaps revealing myself as something of a
heathen.[13]

Once Casement realized the determination of the Catholic Church
to establish a mission among the Indians of the Putumayo, he did not
hesitate to work for a Catholic mission. An office for the fund was set
up with a banker named Percy H. Browne in charge. Browne and
Casement worked together in the campaign to raise 15,000 pounds.
Because the sponsorship of a Catholic mission had proven to be too
sensitive for the Anglican Church, solicitation was being carried out
quietly and privately.

* * *

At the end of May, Genocchi was informed confidentially by
Msgr. Bidwell of the plan to solicit contributions from Protestants as
well as from Catholics and to convince public opinion that only a
Catholic mission had a prospect of success. Bidwell and Casement had
decided to proceed along the following lines: (1) the official papers
would be laid before Parliament by Edward Grey; (2) the press would
comment on them, and stir up public opinion; (3) an appeal would be
issued, signed by several men of different religious convictions,
pointing out that the only remedy lay in the establishment of a mission
in the Putumayo, and that only a Catholic mission would have any
chance of success. Having agreed on the course of action, they set
themselves to working out the details. They would form a committee,
name trustees, get signatures to the appeal, secure the cooperation of
the press, and time all of this with the appearance of the Blue Book.
They had to be ready to face the objection that was sure to be raised by
Protestant Missionary Societies: "We are ready to send out a mission,
and do not see why the mission must be a Catholic one."

The Committee that was set up consisted of: Sir Roger Casement
(Protestant); Mr. Bell (Protestant and one of the Commission sent out
by the British Company to investigate); Count Blucher, Major Pereira,
Mr. Dister Drummond, Mr. Prendergast, Msgr. Bidwell (all Catholics);
Mr. Percy Browne as the Secretary. Count Blucher (a son of Prince
Blucker who married a Stapleton Bretherton, and was a very good

---

[13] R. Casement to Archbishop Randall Davidson, March 13, 1912. National
Library of Ireland (Dublin), 13073 (quoted in *The Lives of Roger Casement*, by B. L. Reid,
[New Haven: Yale University Press, 1976], p. 140-141).

Catholic) and Mr. Pauling (also Catholic, very wealthy, who had organized the railroads in South Africa and China) were named Trustees. The appeal would be signed by the Duke of Hamilton (Scottish Presbyterian), the Duke of Norfolk, Mr. Pauling, Mr. Bell, Mr. William Goschen (Protestant, a son of the late Lord Goschen, and a partner in the firm), Mr. Claude Montefiore (a Jew), and perhaps a few others. All these had studied the appeal and agreed to sign. The appeal stated quite clearly that only a Catholic mission was possible. As was expected, when this was brought to the attention of some of the Nonconformist societies, they immediately objected that there was no reason why they should not send a mission. To settle the matter, Bidwell and Casement appealed to the Foreign Office and obtained an official communication to the effect that only a Catholic mission could possibly succeed. Bidwell hoped not only to ward off further opposition in this way but also to ensure wholehearted support upon circulation of the appeal. At the same time, they worked hard to get the backing and cooperation of the press. In the meantime, the Foreign Office had privately agreed to time the publication of the Blue Book according to the arrangements they had made. Bidwell felt confident that within a few weeks they would collect the 15,000 pounds they were seeking.[14]

On his arrival in London, Genocchi first contacted Cardinal Francis Bourne and his chancellor, Msgr. Bidwell. A meeting with Bidwell, Casement, Browne and Genocchi was arranged for June 19. After the session, Genocchi in accord with Bidwell, Casement, and Browne, sent a telegram to the Secretary of State suggesting that the announcement of the impending encyclical be delayed. He also stated that a report of the conversation was being forwarded. That very day the report was on its way.

In his report Genocchi informed Cardinal Merry del Val that the Protestants, especially the Nonconformists, would like in every way to send a mission to the Putumayo. They were not yet throwing in the towel although it seemed certain that they would not succeed. After the government's release of Casement's reports (which was to be soon), Sir Edward Grey's declaration and other comments of the press would convince the Protestants to desist. Before the reports were released any publication concerning the existence of the encyclical would produce the opposite effect, and would even cause some embarrassment to the English government. By announcing the existence of the pontifical document later, at an opportune moment, it would become evident that the posting of the pontifical letter was prior to the discussion by the

---

[14] M. Bidwell to G. Genocchi, May 25, 1912. ASV.SS. F.4. 146.

house of Commons. The members of the Putumayo Mission Fund committee asked the Cardinal for permission to mention the existence of the letter themselves if circumstances demanded it. Genocchi added that all agreed it would be best to convince the Irish Franciscans as soon as possible. The Irish were preferable to the English Franciscans because the latter were few and less prepared by disposition and training. Furthermore, all the Irish members of Parliament would defend the missionaries, their compatriots, if necessary. Bidwell and others suggested that, in order to avoid any contention on the part of Protestants, it would be wise for the missionaries not to leave from London.[15]

One can readily imagine what Casement and Genocchi shared, aside from these formal and official duties, when they met for the first time. Both had had the terrible experience of witnessing the atrocities committed against the Indians, and both were animated by the same fervent desire to bring these atrocities to an end.

Two days later Genocchi left for Ireland where he met with the Superior of the Franciscans. However, his hopes were not realized. He had noted with Cardinal Merry del Val that the letter which the Father General of the Franciscans gave him for the Irish Franciscans was "not imperative." Genocchi added that, if it was necessary, he would telegraph the Cardinal. If the Cardinal thought it wise, he could answer that Genocchi should insist to the Irish Franciscans that this was the wish of the Holy See.[16] But the good will of the Irish Province was deterred by the many demands on its limited personnel. Genocchi turned to the English Province to assume the greater part of the burden in carrying out the pontifical designs. Despite the scarcity of members in the English province, the Father Provincial, Peter Hickey, found it possible to add the Peruvian mission to his already numerous commitments. He was seconded by the good will of his confreres, more than one of whom offered himself spontaneously for the mission.

[15] G. Genocchi to Cardinal R. Merry del Val, June 19, 1912. ASV.SS. F.4. 143, 144.
[16] G. Genocchi to Cardinal R. Merry del Val, June 19, 1912. ASV.SS. F.4. 145.

CHAPTER X

THE ENCYCLICAL *LACRIMABILI STATU INDORUM*

On June 26, 1912, the encyclical *On the condition of the Indians* was sent to the representatives of the Holy See in Brazil, Argentina, Chile, Peru, Colombia and Mexico, with the recommendation that it be distributed at once to all the bishops of the South American continent:

> Along with this letter I send your Excellency several copies of the encyclical. The Holy Father in conformity with the wise initiative taken by the Holy See last year, once again calls the attention and the concern of the bishops of Latin America to the necessity of endeavoring effectively to promote the civil and religious redemption of the Indians scattered in those territories.[1]

A week later the press learned about the existence of the pontifical document in favor of the Indians. It was just about this time that the English government decided to publish Casement's two reports in a Blue Book. Writing to Cardinal Capecelatro, Genocchi commented:

> The Holy Father's encyclical was announced on time. Today the Foreign Office will distribute to the House of Commons the official reports on the natives of the Putumayo. On Monday the whole English press will be filled with it and the subject will begin to be spoken of in other parts of Europe. It will be evident that the Pope did not await the publication of the English inquiry to attend to those children far away. It will be evident that he too has reports in his possession, which, in one aspect at least, are more complete than those of the English government. Furthermore only the Pope with the Catholic missions can offer the real remedy.

"The subscription for the mission," Genocchi continued, "is not yet begun publicly." The committee of the Putumayo Mission Fund was awaiting the government's declaration first. Nevertheless, 700 pounds had already been collected from several people who had been informed privately. Genocchi told of moves to ward off opposition:

> Today I am going to Downside Abbey (near Bath) where I know the Abbot, and I shall urge him to devote himself seriously to the matter.

---

[1] ASV.SS. F.4. 136.

Yesterday I spoke with one of the heads of the foreign Protestant missions, whom I had already met in Rome. I hope to persuade him to oppose the attempt to establish Protestant missions in the Putumayo. The Anglicans are already persuaded. The Nonconformists are still resisting." [2]

* * *

The English government decided to bring to public attention Casement's two reports and the correspondence with Lima and with Washington from January 1911 to June 1912, when it realized that the Peruvian government hesitated to put an end to the terrible state of affairs in the Putumayo. Ten days after receiving Casement's reports, on January 16, 1911, the Foreign Office instructed the British Minister at Lima to inform the Peruvian government confidentially, and in a friendly manner, of Casement's findings. "His Majesty's government," the Foreign Office added, "is unwilling to publish the facts without first bringing them to the notice of the government primarily concerned, who... will, in the interest of justice and humanity, take steps at once to punish the criminals, and to prevent the continuance or recurrence of the atrocities." [3] At the same time, James Bryce, the British Ambassador in Washington, was sent a copy of Casement's list of criminals. This list was delivered to the American government. On April 21, 1911, the Foreign Office sent a telegram to the British Minister in Lima, requesting information about Peru's attitude. "Only one of the black list criminals," the Foreign Office observed, "had been discovered, and he had been given bail." Most of the others were reported to have escaped. Aguero was even said to have gone out into the Coquetá district with an armed band after burning and destroying what he could in the hope of stirring up the Boras Indians. [4]

At the end of April, 1911, the British Minister at Lima informed the Foreign Office that a number of accused employees had been dismissed, and that Judge Paredes had set out on a gunboat to inquire about the allegations. He would spend three months on his task. Meanwhile it was reported that many of the accused men fled to Manaus on rafts, taking with them some dozens of Huitotos Indians of both sexes, intending to sell them on the Acre River for fifty pounds each.

---

[2] G. Genocchi to Cardinal A. Capecelatro, July 13, 1912, AGG. L.3/C.
[3] *Correspondence respecting the Treatment of British Colonial Subjects and Native Indians employed in the Collection of Rubber in the Putumayo District* (London : Published by His Majesty's Stationary Office, 1912), p. 5.
[4] *Ibid.*, p. 143.

Judge Paredes's inquiry fully confirmed Casement's reports. The Peruvian government had repeatedly made promises of reform to the British Minister at Lima, whose representations had latterly been supported by his American colleague. However, no definitive reform was carried out. Casement returned to Iquitos on a second investigation (August 16, 1911 - February 1912) and reported that no effective steps had been taken either to punish those responsible for the crimes or to prevent their recurrence. The Peruvian government had appointed a commission to outline reforms but its work was constantly delayed.

On February 23, 1912, the English government informed the American government: "We feel that nothing will be done and that no progress will be made without publication of Sir R. Casement's report."[5] One fact proved that no reform was taking place. In a dispatch to Washington, the Foreign Office revealed that the amount of rubber exported from January 1 through April, 1912, equaled the amount of the entire export of 1911. Under these circumstances the only course remaining was to bring the facts to the knowledge of the public opinion.[6]

On July 15, *The Times* printed a thorough summary on the Blue Book under the title "The Putumayo Atrocities: A South American Congo. Sir Roger Casement's Report Published." The article concluded with this statement:

> The best remedy available, apart from government action, would undoubtedly be the establishment of a Roman Catholic mission, and such a mission, if dispatched, should receive the support of all right-minded people without distinction, since no other Christian denomination would be allowed by Peruvian law to undertake a similar task. From official publications issued by the Peruvian government, it is evident that the treatment has already had the attention of the Holy See, which has urged reforms. The Vatican has indeed not confined its good offices in this direction to the natives of Peru, but has made representations of the same nature to other South American governments. No one who reads Sir Roger Casement's reports can fail to wish it means and power to extend its civilizing influence. The existing system cries aloud to Heaven.

The following day the same newspaper published the appeal drawn up during the meeting that Genocchi had with Casement, Browne and

---

[5] *Ibid.*, p. 143-144.

[6] *Ibid.*, p. 160. An abridged version of the report of Judge Paredes was published in the United States Official Publication, *Slavery in Peru* (Washington: House of Representatives' Document, 1913).

Bidwell. The appeal was signed by Hamilton, W. H. Goschen, W. Yoynson, Norfolk and E. Seymour Bell.

> The condition of affairs disclosed in the Parliamentary Paper dealing with the region known as the Putumayo on the Upper Amazon, where the primitive Indian tribes have been so ruthlessly ill-treated by agents of a company that has its headquarters in England, must fill the minds of all with sentiments of profound pity and compassion.
>
> It is true that the Peruvian government, which has had its attention called to the grave abuses, is trying to remedy them. But the district is a very remote one, and the efforts of the Executive must, of necessity, be primarily directed to administrative work, and it is to be feared that, unless collaboration is forthcoming from outside humanitarian sources, the last remnants of these unfortunate people will speedily disappear.
>
> While there are doubtless many people in this country who would wish to entrust any remedial undertaking to a Protestant body, it must be borne in mind that, according to the Peruvian Constitution, work of this kind could only be permitted if entrusted to the Roman Catholic Church. It is therefore suggested that a Roman Catholic mission should be sent to the Putumayo, far away though it is, and difficult as any work carried on under such conditions must be. For years to come the operations of these missionaries must consist, less of abstract religious propaganda, than of human fellowship inspired by compassion and the desire to uplift and benefit materially. For this large sums will be required, both initially and in the direction of providing an annual income, but in view of the expenditure the Church is itself prepared to make, a sum of 15,000 pounds will ensure the definitive establishment of a Christian mission on the Putumayo.
>
> We therefore appeal for this sum, not only to members of the Roman Catholic Church, but to all those whose hearts may in any way have been touched by the recital of one of the most terrible tragedies which has resulted from the commercialism of our time.

The importance of Genocchi's work in this affair will be better appreciated in the light of the violent opposition awakened. This opposition came from both the Protestants in England who were against the Catholic mission and from the Peruvians who were averse to the English nationality of the missionaries. Genocchi worked energetically and tirelessly on behalf of the Holy See to get the mission accomplished. He was loyally supported by the British government in London.

* * *

At first the English press was benevolent, without exception, towards the proposal of a Catholic mission. Just two days after the publication of Casement's report, the Canon of Westminster Abbey,

Hensley H. Henson, wrote: "I have read through the Blue Book on the infamies which have been and are proceeding in the Putumayo district of Peru." He desired to express the hope that a "generous response" would be made to the Duke of Norfolk's appeal. In view of such an abomination there could be no question of denominational distinction. "The Roman Catholic Church has clearly this duty laid on her, and all Christians have as clearly the duty on them of facilitating her work." [7]

Genocchi cabled Cardinal Merry del Val: "The appeal of the committee is very well received by the press, which insists on the exclusiveness of our mission." Official Peruvian telegrams tried to prove that the crimes were "a thing of the past." The English press published documents proving the contrary and argued that "a Catholic mission is the only remedy." [8] However, it was not long before the press began, here and there, to raise discordant notes of reservation, doubt, and even protest. They raised the following question: was it indeed true that the mission must necessarily be a Catholic one? Should Protestant missionaries resign themselves to non-intervention in the Putumayo? In an undertaking of such great moral import, why should the way be left open only to Catholics? Indeed would it not be better, in a humanitarian question such as this, to permit Protestants as well as Catholics to come to the aid of the Indians?

On July 19, the problem was brought before the English government. In the House of Commons, Mr. King asked the Secretary of State for the Foreign Office whether a Roman Catholic mission to Peru would receive help, advice, and encouragement from the Foreign Office and from the English representative abroad, whereas a Protestant mission would not. If this were the case, he asked, was there any precedent for the Foreign Office to favor one Christian denomination over another? Mr. Acland answered that the Foreign Office was "not directly concerned" with the dispatch of religious missions to Putumayo. He would, of course, give as much assistance as would be possible or advisable. The Peruvian constitution did not permit the public exercise of any religion except the Roman Catholic one. The Secretary of State was informed that missions of other denominations would not be accorded the necessary facilities by the Peruvian authorities. With political realism the Secretary of State added:

> In determining the mission to support, it is rather important to select the missions which will have the best chance of getting something done. I think the question between the particular religion which will be rep-

---

[7] *The Times*, July 17, 1912.
[8] G. Genocchi to Cardinal R. Merry del Val, July 16, 1912. ASV.SS. F.4. 165.

resented by the mission ought to be entirely subordinate to that, and it is undoubtedly the fact that a Roman Catholic mission has a far better chance of getting something done than any other mission that could be sent. ... Any application for facilities for a Protestant mission to the Putumayo would probably meet with an answer similar to that received in 1907, when a project was entertained by the Baptist Missionary Society of sending a mission to the Peruvian Amazon.[9]

On that occasion the Peruvian government expressed its inability to accede to the desire of the Society because it was in opposition to the terms of the Peruvian constitution. This forbade the public exercise of any religion except the Roman Catholic.

At one point, a letter to the press was written by the Anglican bishop of the Falkland Islands. He had nominal jurisdiction over the whole of South America and happened to be in London at this time. Writing in *The Daily Mail*, the bishop declared that Iquitos, the center from which rubber traders worked in the Putumayo, was part of his diocese. According to his plan, Iquitos was one of the places where he wished to start a center of Christian work. He was sure that he could find the men, "strong, manly, forceful Christians of the very type required." The bishop stated that "really first-class chaplains, schools, nursing homes and English doctors be established." He added that he had been in touch with the Peruvian government and could confidently count on their sympathy and help in forwarding the work of his Church, as both the President in Lima and the Minister in London, *Señor* Eduardo Lembeke, personally expressed to him "their warm appreciation" for his scheme.[10]

Because the Peruvian constitution forbade public activities of any religion other than the Catholic one, it should have been clear that the courteous words of the President of Peru to the Anglican bishop had no value other than that of mere words. Later on, the Foreign Minister of Peru, C. Leguia y Partinez, explicitly denied the report that the President of Peru and the Peruvian Minister in London had promised to accept a protestant mission in Peru. The newspaper, *The Star*, July 25, pointed out two geographical facts which "the good bishop's evangelical fervor had caused him to overlook." One was that the Bishop's headquarters of the Falkland Islands were about 6,000 miles from Iquitos and therefore hardly the nearest work at hand. Secondly, a mission in Iquitos would have the same effect on the savage horrors of the Putumayo region "as a mission in, say, Fenchurch-Street would

---

[9] *The Times*, July 20, 1912.
[10] *The Daily Mail*, July 25, 1912.

have on the condition of affairs in St. Kilda." [11] Iquitos was merely the store for Putumayo rubber. As no atrocities were committed in Iquitos, a sufficient reason did not exist to call the bishop 6,000 miles from the Falkland Islands. The region where the atrocities occurred was an eight days' journey up the Amazon, Putumayo, and Igaraparaná rivers. It was a country extending over 10,000 square miles.

In the columns of *The Times* dating July 27, the Putumayo Mission Fund committee stressed that all Protestants with experience of the place were equally agreed that the mission had to be Catholic if it was to meet the real needs of the situation. Casement also intervened in the debate, publicly supporting the establishment of a Roman Catholic mission. On July 31, *The Times* published his statement: "I have no doubt that the readiest means are to be found through the agency of the Roman Catholic Church, and every other person who knows the region is of the same opinion." There is no doubt that his position was dictated by a political realism, but probably his new religious attitude was not foreign to his statement. It was at this time that Casement began to be drawn to the Catholic Church because of the opposition of the Anglicans towards the sponsorship of a Roman Catholic mission, when the Holy See had taken a firm stand concerning the problem of the Indians. Born of a Protestant father and a Catholic mother Casement was educated in Protestant schools and passed for Protestant. However, his mother had him secretly baptized a Catholic. On June 29, 1911, Casement published a letter in *The Nation* and signed himself "A Catholic Reader." Furthermore he wrote to his friends, the McVeaghs: "I am more Catholic than anything else."

* * *

During this last and most delicate phase of his work, Genocchi kept a watchful eye on the press, made the utmost use of all sources of information and exerted his influence in all quarters. He took the greatest possible advantage from the situation that had arisen. While the Putumayo Mission Fund committee replied to the Anglican bishop and others, he himself took advantage of the Anglican bishop's letter to eliminate any further delay. It was necessary to act quickly to make the Catholic mission an accomplished fact. On July 19, Genocchi cabled Cardinal Merry del Val: "Dissidents object our missionaries would be Peruvian. Needing reply I spoke to English Provincial who agreed we appoint English Franciscans now." Because the German press (Catholic

---

[11] Fenchurch Street is in central London and St. Kilda is a small island in the Hebrides off the West coast of Scotland.

press included) took the pretext of the publication of Casement's report to make England responsible for the atrocities committed against the Indians, Genocchi added this request in his telegram: "I would ask you consider immediate anti-British interpretation German newspaper even Catholic. Obtaining legitimate correction would make excellent impression." [12]

The English Provincial of the Franciscans saw the situation as clearly as Genocchi did. He quickly and gladly accomplished all that the Apostolic Visitor asked on behalf of the Holy See. He accepted the Putumayo mission and designated the following priests as missionaries: Leo Sambrook, Frederick Furlong, Felix Ryan and Cyprian Byrne. This decision, communicated at once to the press, put an end to the activities of those Protestants who wanted to send their own missionaries in Peru. *The Times* of July 20, published the names of the missionaries after the following statement:

> Several months ago the Pope instructed the bishops in South America to occupy themselves with greater zeal with the protection of the Indians. Padre Genocchi, of the Mission of the Sacred Heart, was sent to inquire into the situation on the spot. Later on the atrocities committed on the rubber estates in Peru became known, and the Peruvian government petitioned the Pope that fresh Catholic missions should be established in the districts where these atrocities were being perpetrated so that the missionaries might keep the Peruvian government informed of what was going on. The scheme met with the support of all Catholics and of a number of influential Protestants, who likewise sent contributions in money to the Holy See in aid of the proposed missions. The Pope was greatly moved and made arrangements with the Peruvian Minister to the Holy See and with Padre Genocchi for the establishment of missions in

---

[12] G. Genocchi to Cardinal R. Merry del Val, July 19, 1912. ASV.SS. 59660. *The Times* issues of July 18, 19 and 22 quoted the comments of several German newspapers.

The *Berliner Neueste Nachrichten* used the phrase: "English butchers of Indians."

The *Reichsbote* on July 18 wrote: "It is scarcely credible that human nature, and, above all, the members of a nation like the British, which aspires to be regarded as the champion of humanity, could be capable of such infamy. Thirty thousand people were slaughtered in six years from pure love of cruelty.... These butcheries remain an indelible blot on the British name."

The *Kölnische Volkszeitung*, the most important Catholic newspaper in Germany, on July 16, published a telegram from London which read: "The British Consul General in Peru has published a Blue-book containing sensational revelation concerning atrocities practised by the English on Peruvians."

The *Germania*, another Catholic newspaper, on July 18, after quoting R. Casement's report, wrote: "Thus writes a Briton about Britons. The Biblemen who set the whole world in commotion over the alleged Congo atrocities and calumniated Catholic Belgium have now a fruitful soil for their labours."

the district of the Putumayo. The Pope's final action was to address an encyclical letter to all Bishops in South America exhorting them to protect the Indians in their respective dioceses.

Pleased with the success, Pope Pius X sent a wire expressing his satisfaction to the English Franciscans and he imparted his blessing to the missionaries who had been chosen.[13]

* * *

On August 5, Cardinal Merry del Val cabled Genocchi: "This evening the known document is published."[14] The nations of the world, already moved by the press accounts of the atrocities against the Indians, were moved still more by the Holy Father's strong protest and expression of horror and sorrow.

The encyclical, which began with the words *Lacrimabili Statu Indorum*, recalled the December 22, 1741, letter of Benedict XIV, who was greatly moved by the deplorable condition of the Indians in South America and pleaded their cause "in most weighty words." He lamented that:

> Men of the orthodox faith who, as if they had utterly forgotten all sense of the charity poured forth in our hearts by the Holy Spirit, presumed to reduce the wretched Indians, without the light of faith and even those who had been washed in the laver of regeneration, to servitude, or to sell them as slaves to others, or to deprive them of their property, and to treat them with such inhumanity that they were thus greatly hindered from embracing the Christian faith, and most strongly moved to regard it with abhorrence.

Pius X declared that he had to deplore in many places almost the same things which Benedict XIV complained about. However, the "worst of these indignities," meaning slavery, was abolished. Although much had been done for the Indians, Pius X declared, "There is much more that still remains to be done." At this point the Pope spoke in strong terms to denounce the cruelties committed against the Indians.

> When we consider the crimes and outrages still committed against the Indians, our heart is filled with horror, and we are moved to great

---

[13] "Beatissimus Pater iucundo accepit animo nunnullos ex ista religiosa familia sese missioni Putumayo volentes addiscisse, iisdemque jam nunc Apostolicam libenter impertit benedictionem." Cardinal R. Merry del Val to Fr. P. Hickey, August 8, 1912. St. Anthony's Archives, Forest Gate, London.

[14] Cardinal R. Merry del Val to G. Genocchi, August 5, 1912. ASV.SS. F.5. 3.

compassion for this unhappy race. For what can be so cruel and so barbarous as to scourge men and brand them with hot iron, often for the most trivial causes, often for mere lust of cruelty; or, having suddenly overthrown them, to slay hundreds or thousands in one unceasing massacre; or to waste villages and districts and slaughter the inhabitants, so that some tribes, as we understand, have become extinct in these last few years? The lust of gain has done much to make the minds of men so barbarous. ... And as they are removed from the habits of religion and the vigilance of the State, and in a measure even from civil society, it easily comes to pass that those who have not already come there with evil morals soon begin to be corrupted, and then, when all bonds of right and duty are broken, they fall away into all hateful vices. Nor in this do they take any pity on the weakness of sex and age; so that we are ashamed to mention the crimes and outrages they commit in seeking out and selling women and children, wherein it may be truly said that they have surpassed the worst examples of pagan iniquity.

The Pope went on to say that when reports of these matters were first brought to his attention, for a time he was unable to believe that atrocities of such enormity could possibly be perpetrated. But after he had been assured by abundant witnesses, by the Delegates of the Apostolic See, by the missionaries, and by other men "wholly worthy of belief," he could no longer have any doubt about the truth of these declarations. He acknowledged that "those who bear rule in these republics were making every effort to remove this glaring disgrace and this stain from their states." At the same time, the Pope did not hesitate to say this about the civil powers: "Whether from the cunning of the criminals who speedily cross the frontiers, or through the neglect of action or deception on the part of officials, they often did little good and sometimes nothing." But if the "work of the Church is added to the work of the state, then at length the desired fruit shall be obtained in greater abundance." Therefore the Pope was calling upon the Bishops to give "special care and thought" to this case, which was in every way worthy of their pastoral office and duty.

We particularly urge you to foster and promote all the good works instituted in your diocese for the benefit of the Indians, and to see that other works likely to contribute to this end might be instituted. In the next place you will diligently admonish your flocks on their most sacred duty of helping religious missions to the natives who first inhabited the American soil. Let them know that they ought to help this work especially in two ways, to wit, by their gifts and by their prayers; and that it is not only their religion, but their country also, that asks this of them. Do you, moreover, take care that wheresoever moral instruction is given, in seminaries, in colleges, in convent schools, and more especially

in the churches, Christian charity, which holds all men, without
distinction of nation or color, as true brethren, shall be continually
preached and commended. And this charity must be made manifest not
so much by words as by deeds. Moreover, every opportunity must be
taken to show what a great dishonor is done to the Christian name by
these base deeds, which we are here denouncing.

As for his part, if he received the consent and support of the public
authorities,the Pope was planning to extend the field of apostolic work
in those broad regions. He wanted to appoint further missionary
stations where the Indians could find safety and succor. The Pope
described the Catholic Church as "a fertile mother of apostolic men,
who pressed by the charity of Christ, are brought to give their life for
the brethren." He thought it well to use these men where the need was
greatest, "in order to deliver the Indians from the slavery of Satan and
of wicked men." In order that the Bishops' work for the benefit of the
Indians might be even more efficacious, the Pope condemned and
declared the following to be guilty of grave crime:

> Whosoever shall dare or presume to reduce the said Indians to slavery,
> to sell them, to buy them, to exchange or give them, to separate them
> from their wives and children, to deprive them of goods, and chattels, to
> transport or send them to other places, or in any way whatsoever to rob
> them of freedom and hold them in slavery; or to give counsel, help,
> favor, and work on any pretext of colour to them that do these things,
> or to preach or teach that it is lawful, or to cooperate therewith in any
> way whatever.

Accordingly the Pope declared that "the power of absolving
penitents in the sacramental tribunal from these crimes shall be reserved
to the local Ordinaries." [15]

* * *

In his August 8 report to Cardinal Merry del Val, Genocchi gave
the minutes of the meeting held by the English Franciscans the
preceding day during which they officially decided to accept the mission
in the Putumayo. "The Fathers in this definitory most willingly
accepted the wish of the Holy See expressed in the Most Reverend
Minister General's letter. From the Fathers who volunteered, four,

---

[15] *Acta Apostolicae Sedis*, 4 (1912), p. 521-528. The English translation is found in
Claudia Carlen, IHM, *The Papal Encyclicals* (1903-1939) (McGrath Publishing Company,
1981), p. 131-133.

Father Leo Sambrook, Frederick Furlong, Felix Ryan and Cyprian Byrne, were chosen to undertake the work of evangelizing the mission known as the Putumayo." [16]

Their departure was scheduled for November. With this Genocchi considered his mission in England accomplished and notified the Secretary of State that he was ready to leave England. On August 14, the Secretary of State cabled: "Received report of August 8. Scheduled departure for November fine. Nothing opposes your return to Rome if you think prolonging stay in England unnecessary." [17]

Genocchi arrived in Rome August 20. There he published an article entitled "The New Mission in the Putumayo, Upper Peru," in the Vatican newspaper *L'Osservatore Romano*. For the Italian readers, Genocchi reviewed the American and English press accounts which dealt with the problem of the Putumayo. He showed the need and importance of the action undertaken by Pope Pius X for the redemption of the Indians.

A United States Catholic review, *America*, contained an article on the Putumayo by the Jesuit M. Kenny in the August, 1912 issue. Genocchi quoted the first two paragraphs in their entirety and summarized the rest.

> The publication by Sir Roger Casement, British Commissioner, of the terrible brutalities inflicted by the officials of a London rubber Company on the Indians in the Putumayo district of Peru, was promptly followed by the statement that religion alone could supply the remedy and only Catholic missionaries could exercise religious influence on the Indians. Accordingly an appeal has been made to the benevolent for sufficient funds to establish and maintain Catholic missions in the Putumayo. It is a striking coincidence, that early in 1911, more than a year before Sir Roger Casement had issued his report, Pope Pius X had also sent a Commissioner, Father Genocchi, of the Sacred Heart of Jesus, to inquire into the condition of the Indians, not merely in Peru, but in all the States of South America, and his account not only confirms the British Commissioner's, but shows that the outrages cover a still wider area.
>
> His report has not been published, but a letter, dated February 11, contained this passage: "The search for rubber, which is here called black gold, has given rise to worse abuses in these districts than in the Congo. In some parts of South America, in spite of the laws, the most shameful slavery prevails, with massacres, sales, atrocious tortures, and every other iniquity of which brutalized and degenerate man is capable when free from the control of law. The Catholic missions, the only

---

[16] G. Genocchi to Cardinal R. Merry del Val, August 8, 1912. ASV.SS. F.5. 23.
[17] Cardinal R. Merry del Val to G. Genocchi, August 14, 1912. ASV.SS. F.5. 4.

barrier to the wholesale destruction of the Indians, are lacking where they are most urgently needed. For this the Holy Father wishes to make provision, and the idea is worthy of the highest praise."

His Holiness had, in fact, done so before the Putumayo outrages were given to the world. No sooner had Father Genocchi returned to Rome and made his report in person, than Pius X embodied its contents in an encyclical to the archbishops and bishops of South America, directing them to bend all their energies — by their personal exertions, through religious organizations, and by cooperation with the various States in any movement for the protection of the Indians — to the correction of abuses and the promotion of moral and social betterment of that oppressed and much neglected people.

Sir Roger Casement and his fellow-commissioners looked for reform to the same sources for they regard the Roman Catholic mission as the sole feasible step that can be taken by those interested on humanitarian grounds in the welfare of the Indians. That non-Catholics should so conclude has shocked some good people among us; but it will astonish no one who is acquainted with the historical association of that locality. These should be known to a wide circle of non-Catholic as well as Catholic readers.

Here the Jesuit spoke of the early missions of his Society, quoting from the Italian historian Ludovico Muratori and several Protestant historians. He went on to speak of the evangelization of Brazil and other regions of South America and discussed the establishment of the first Reduction of Loreto up to the destruction of the missions by the bigoted Marquis of Pombal. He cited the remark of a Protestant named Cunningham Graham regarding the missions among the South American Indians before 1767, when the missionaries were being dragged off in chains from the territories where they had been working for almost two centuries: "Let the zeal of any class of men be what it may; if they oppose themselves to slavery, and, at the same time, are reported to have lands in which is gold, and resolutely exclude adventurers from them, their doom is sealed." Father Kenny then concluded: "This outline of the rise and fall of the greatest of all Indian missionary enterprises will give a general idea of what should be done, and what should be avoided in the establishment and maintenance of effective Catholic missions among the Indians."

The Times of August 5, 1912, published a sermon delivered by Hensley Henson, Canon of Westminster Abbey. Explaining the Gospel of the Liturgy of the day, the Canon placed particular stress on the text of Luke 16:9, "I tell you, make friends for yourselves by means of the unrighteous mammon, so that when it fails they may receive you into the eternal habitations." Genocchi commented:

Unfortunately, many men, instead of employing money to make friends of the poor, and to propitiate heaven, justify the words of Jesus Christ, who calls wealth unrighteous mammon, i.e., often fruit of injustice and incentive to injustice. A worthy example is the horrendous story of rubber collectors in the Amazon region, especially in the area where the Putumayo passes through. Even elsewhere, in South America, in Africa, in Mexico, atrocities are committed, but, as far as we know, they are not as many nor as diabolic as they are in the Putumayo. All Englishmen already know enough about it since the publication of the Blue Book and the articles of the press. England, following its humanitarian tradition, does not fail to act through its government, putting into practice the means at its disposal, to relieve the world of the shame of such slavery and such barbarity.

Genocchi recorded this long passage from the sermon of Canon Hensley Henson:

But while these necessary changes are being effected in the law, the miserable remnant of the native population is being destroyed by the vile brutalities which this Blue Book has disclosed. Something must be done at once if this great iniquity is not to be accomplished. The prompt action of the governments of Great Britain and the United States might effect something (and in order that such action may be taken there is urgent need that public opinion should show itself insistent on the subject), but political action must be slow, and can at best be only temporary. There is need of another kind of action if the hand of the oppressor is to be arrested, and his victims relieved and rescued. Sir Roger Casement, who has fully earned the right to direct us, holds that the establishment of a Christian mission in the Putumayo district would be organized and carried on by the Roman Catholic Church. This opinion has been publicly endorsed by Sir Edward Grey. I hope that many English Churchmen will send contributions to the fund, which has been opened by the Duke of Norfolk and others, in order to raise without delay the sum (15,000 pounds) which is said to be required. It has been officially announced that the projected mission is to be entrusted to the English Franciscans, an arrangement which will undoubtedly give satisfaction in this country. This is no time, when the Indians are perishing, to debate the merits of Churches and to inflame the mind with the recollections of ecclesiastical differences and conflicts. For my part, I prefer to recall the glorious achievements of Roman Catholic missionaries in the past and in the present. I refuse to see in them any other character than that of fellow-Christians called to an urgent and difficult work. I rejoice to aid their effort, and I pray God to bless it.

The Truth, the weekly London review, was the first to sound the alarm about the Putumayo horrors. To keep public opinion awake in

England, it had published an appalling anthology in the issue dated August 7, 1912. Genocchi recounted a few passages concerning the atrocities committed against Indians "to let the readers better understand the Holy Father's concern in assisting the poor Indians with missionaries and other means." He concluded:

> This is enough. Too much has been gleaned from this terrible anthology. Just think that in the past ten years, in the region of the Putumayo alone, no less than 30,000 poor Indians were barbarously slaughtered. The government of Peru and of the other neighboring republics were impotent to prevent such outrageous barbarities because of the distance and the unrest in these places.

Genocchi stated: "With the help of the missionaries sent by Pius X and the stimulus of the great powers, especially England, we hope that justice will triumph, and the charity of Jesus Christ will heal the bleeding and putrid wounds which still infect the exalted civilization of our century." [18]

---

[18] *L'Osservatore Romano*, October 31, 1912.

CHAPTER XI

THE HOLY SEE AND THE PERUVIAN GOVERNMENT

When Genocchi returned to Rome on August 20, it seemed that the project of the Catholic mission was settled. However, clouds appeared, this time on the Peruvian horizon. Political complications arose. Genocchi informed Cardinal Capecelatro that he had to go to the Secretariate of State quite often, because, as he said, "Peru resents England and does not want English missionaries. But we shall get what we want." [1]

The publication of Casement's report had given rise to a general explosion of indignation among all civilized peoples. Peru defended itself by pointing out the difficulties of supervising the Putumayo, due to the international dispute between Peru, Colombia and Brazil over the territorial boundaries. Furthermore, Peru accused the English rubber company of being solely responsible for the atrocities committed against the Indians. The Peruvian press attacked the interference of the British and United States governments. A series of articles entitled "Through the Putumayo," appeared in *La Prensa* signed by a *Señor* Gutiérrez de Quintanilla, head of the Historical Museum in Lima. The headings of the articles are sufficient to indicate the nature of their contents: "Traditional Hatreds," "Failing Humanitarian Methods, Armed Defense," "The International Scandal Lacks Reformatory Efficacy: It is the Beginning of Spoliation," "Greater Barbarities in the Dominions of England, France, and the Anglo-American United States," "Are We Peruvians the Only Criminals in the Putumayo? Territorial Expansion, Hypocrisy," "The Sovereignty of Peru and the Hypocrisy of 'Dreadnoughts'," "International Cannibalism in the Putumayo," "We are Smoothing the Path for Our Enemies," "The European and Anglo-American Wolves and the Ewes of Spanish Origin," "Colombia in the Putumayo," "Ecuador in the Putumayo," "Common Defense of the Spanish American People."

In an issue of the newspaper *El Comercio* a lengthy communication signed by "Garón" attacked the Leguia Administration for having permitted foreign intervention in violation of the sovereignty of Peru.

---

[1] G. Genocchi to Cardinal A. Capecelatro, October 25, 1912. AGG. L.3/C.

It affirmed that the Peruvian government should have adopted the
patriotic attitude of Venezuela at the time of conflict with the Powers
in 1903. The author strongly defended the Casa Arana which "owes
nothing" to the government of Peru. On the contrary, it was no
mystery for any Loretan that if Colombia was not at that time in
possession of the Putumayo, this was "exclusively due" to the
following: the respect inspired by the members of the armed
employees of the Casa Arana, their determination and patriotism, and
their practical acquaintance with the region and knowledge of the
strategic points which they would occupy at the right time. Those
employees had the advantage of numerous facilities. The Casa Arana
had an abundance of money, food and rapid transportation. They
owned expensive passenger steamers and a greater number of launches
than any commercial enterprise on the rivers. The author concluded:
"And this is the Firm against whose principal partner, *Señor* Arana, an
order of arrest has been issued for a crime which his employees, not
himself, may have committed, the crime of not having allowed
themselves to be eaten by the cannibals of that region." In order to
illustrate the dangers of living in the region and the cannibal habits of
the natives, the article gave many quotations from Rabuchon's notes.
It ended by stating; "Far indeed from meriting the blame of any man,
the *señores* Arana are worthy of the esteem of all reasonable people,
and have earned the gratitude of the nation." [2]

Under these circumstances it is understandable that both
Peruvian public opinion and the Peruvian government could see an
additional offense to national honor in the English nationality of the
missionaries. At first the Peruvian government informed the
Apostolic Delegate in Lima that it would grant facilities to a mission
with a personnel of any nationality, provided it be sent directly
under the responsibility of the Holy See. [3] Subsequently the Peruvian
government had taken exception to terms of the Encyclical letter,
addressed by the Pope to the South American Episcopate. It charged
the Vatican with having an understanding with the English
government as to the publication of the Encyclical at the same time
as the Blue Book and thereby aiding the pro-Colombian press
campaign against Peru. In view of this, Peru's Minister for Foreign
Affairs informed Msgr. Scapardini that "the Peruvian government
would not consent to grant facilities for, or permit access to the

---

[2] Cf. C. De Graz to E. Grey, February 7, 1913. PRO.FO. 12666.
[3] Msgr. A. Scapardini to Cardinal R. Merry del Val, August 16, 1912. ASV.SS.
F.5. 54.

Putumayo of a mission even if sent by the Pope, should it be composed of British subjects." [4]

* * *

On September 9, 1912, the Peruvian government contacted the Holy See through its Chargé d'Affaires. Msgr. Eugenio Pacelli, the future Pope Pius XII, conveyed to Genocchi the report of the conversation that he had with the Peruvian Diplomat.

> The Peruvian Chargé d'Affaires came to tell me that he received a dispatch from the Minister, Mr. Goyeneche. In it Mr. Goyeneche expresses the desire that his government be informed a short time before the Holy See would send the mission to the Putumayo. Moreover, the same Minister, although he does not have instructions about this from the government, but motivated by the desire that the mission have the best possible result, believes that it is necessary to call the attention of the Cardinal Secretary of State to these two points: (1) that it would not seem appropriate for the mission to be composed principally of Englishmen because, after the exaggerated (he says) revelations about the crimes of the Putumayo, that could offend the feelings not of the Minister nor of the government but of the masses and produce some discontent; (2) that the donations which are collected from the Duke of Norfolk and others in England, be given a form such that they do not offend the same national sentiments. [5]

Four days later, on September 13, the Peruvian Chargé d'Affaires returned to the Secretariate of State to say that his government believed that it would be opportune if the missionaries of the Putumayo were exclusively Spanish and not English.

> The Spaniards know the language of the country, have already proven themselves and have other missionaries in Peru. Peru recognizes the very lofty aims of the Holy See and indeed is grateful to it for the benefits of evangelization, but it cannot say the same for England which has imperialistic aims. Anticipating, therefore, difficulties which could arise, the Minister prefers that the Missionaries not be English. For example, it could happen that a missionary is killed by the savages. England could use this as a pretext to intervene, accusing the Peruvian government of not knowing how to protect the security of the English subjects. Today the Monroe Doctrine is in force all over America; but who knows? Things could change. Thus, the Minister, though he recognizes the disinterested and very lofty aims of the Holy See, cannot fail to consider this purely religious aspect alongside the political element as well. [6]

---

[4] Msgr. A. Scapardini to L. Jerome, June 11, 1912. PRO.FO. 45658.
[5] ASV.SS. F.5. 69.
[6] ASV.SS. F.5. 70.

The role played by Genocchi in this circumstance is recorded in the instructions the Secretary of State sent to the Apostolic Delegate in Lima on September 21, 1912. Genocchi's quick insight and sound judgment promptly found both a better appreciation of the circumstances and a more realistic view. He appealed to the interest of the Republic of Peru itself. In England the publication of the Blue Book on the Putumayo atrocities had raised an outcry and created a great stir. Genocchi asked, was it not obvious that only the testimony of English witnesses could persuade the government and people of England that such atrocities no longer in fact existed? The presence of English missionaries at La Chorrera would spare Peru the embarrassment of further protests by the British government and demands on behalf of the Protestant Church of England. These protests and demands would certainly continue in hostile and obstinate fashion unless the excited and angry British nation knew that its own sons were there. The British would trust their missionaries to guard against further barbarities and to protect its own good name which was involved in the famous Peruvian-Amazon Company, largely under British control. In reality then, the Holy See was rendering a true service to Catholic Peru in sending English Franciscans to La Chorrera. The mission of the Putumayo would be absolutely detached from politics since it would be directly dependent on the Holy See for the erection and maintenance of the mission. It would have none but a religious and humanitarian scope, even though conducted by foreign missionaries. These would receive such instructions that their absolute neutrality would be guaranteed. Furthermore, there would be at least one Franciscan from the Ucayali added to their community who would go with them to La Chorrera from Iquitos. Genocchi urged that if such arguments seemed sound, it should not be regarded as less reasonable that the Putumayo mission should depend directly upon the Holy See and not upon local ecclesiastical authorities. In the territory involved, the rights of Colombia overlapped with those of Peru. The absolute neutrality of the Holy See would avoid even the appearance of recognizing the authority of either of the contestants over its mission in disputed areas.[7]

* * *

In a telegram of October 2, Cardinal Merry del Val instructed the Vatican representative to inform officially the Peruvian government and the Prefect Apostolic of San León de Amazonas of the decision of the

---

[7] See letter of Cardinal R. Merry del Val to Msgr. A. Scapardini, September 21, 1912. ASV.DP. F.4. 67, 75.

Holy Father. He intended to erect a new mission in the Putumayo, taking from the Apostolic Prefecture of San León de Amazonas the territory placed on the left bank of the rivers Aguarico, Napo and Amazon at the point where this last enters Brazil. "The other boundaries are not indicated in order not to be prejudicial to the dispute existing between Peru and Colombia. The new mission will be entrusted to the Franciscans of the Leonine Union, and they will have as their place of residence La Chorrera." [8]

In the meantime, the Apostolic Delegate in Colombia, Msgr. Francesco Ragonesi, notified the Holy See on September 27 of some apprehensions of the Colombian government. "This government, fearing that the mission sent to the Putumayo by the Holy Father may come to an understanding with the Peruvian government and, consequently, may set a precedent contrary to its rights concerning that region, requests that the mission be neutral." [9] Cardinal Merry del Val (on the same day that he informed the Apostolic Delegate at Lima about the erection of the mission in the Putumayo) replied to Msgr. Ragonesi with this instruction: "You can assure this government that the erection of the mission of the Putumayo will be conceived in such terms that in no way will it be prejudicial to the question concerning the boundaries existing between Peru and Colombia." [10]

On October 3 the Apostolic Delegate at Lima personally delivered a diplomatic note to the Minister of Foreign Affairs informing him about the erection of the new mission. The Minister received the note and promised to study the question, which, he said, was "very serious," before giving an answer. In a subsequent meeting, the Minister complained that the Peruvian government was informed only about the erection of the mission and this as late as October 3. In comparison, the English press had known about the creation of the mission a month before and also other details, including names of the missionaries.[11] The Apostolic Delegate had several negotiations with other members of the government, who were involved in the question, without receiving a clear and explicit statement concerning the attitude of Peru towards the

---

[8] Cardinal R. Merry del Val to Msgr. A. Scapardini, October 2, 1912. ASV.DP. F.4. 76.

[9] Msgr. Ragonesi to Cardinal R. Merry del Val, September 27, 1912. ASV.SS. F.5. 73.

[10] Cardinal R. Merry del Val to Msgr. Ragonesi, October 2, 1912. ASV.SS. F.5. 75.

[11] Msgr. A. Scapardini to Cardinal R. Merry del Val, November 10, 1912. ASV.SS. F.6. 27.

new mission. On October 28, in a telegram to the Apostolic Delegate, Cardinal Merry del Val sent the following diplomatic instruction:

> Response is urgently required regarding dispositions of the Peruvian government towards Catholic mission Putumayo. Missionaries' departure would be next November 12. Must have certainty that government would give warm reception establishing missionaries in designated territory. If government should obstruct mission, Holy See would be obliged to publish its failure, declining responsibility. *Odium* would fall on Peruvian government, arousing new ferment in Anglo-Saxon world and would furnish pretext of greater Protestant intervention against Peru's national interest.[12]

Twelve days later the Apostolic Delegate cabled the answer of the Peruvian government to Cardinal Merry del Val, stating also that a report concerning the negotiations would follow: "After much questioning the government finally replies that it accepts the mission but by providing as soon as possible the foundation of the Loreto diocese with the see in Iquitos." [13]

On November 15 and 16, Colombia's Minister to the Holy See sent two notes to Cardinal Merry del Val. In the first, he expressed the feeling of satisfaction and gratitude with which Colombia received the encyclical *Lacrimabili Statu Indorum*. The second note enclosed a pamphlet concerning the responsibility for the deplorable actions which had taken place in the Putumayo. The hidden intention of the Minister appeared evident: to involve the Holy See in the political problem of the sovereignty of the Putumayo. Cardinal Merry del Val at once cabled the Apostolic Delegate in Colombia instructing him to communicate the following to the Colombian government: "A mission in the Putumayo is erected by a decree of the Sacred Congregation for the Propagation of the Faith: the mission has a center La Chorrera, and extends to the left bank of the rivers Aguarico, Napo and Amazon towards La Chorrera, and surrounding territories." The Cardinal pointed out that such delimitation left the dispute concerning the boundaries unprejudiced. Through Mr. Carmelo Arango, the Holy See had learned with satisfaction about the offer of the Colombian government to help the new mission. However, the Cardinal added, it was "necessary" that every eventual monetary help reach the mission through the Holy See.[14]

---

[12] Cardinal R. Merry del Val to Msgr. A. Scapardini, October 28, 1912. ASV.DP. F.4. 77.

[13] Msgr. a. Scapardini to Cardinal R. Merry del Val, November 9, 1912. ASV.SS. F.6. 116.

[14] Cardinal R. Merry del Val to Msgr. Ragonesi, November 18, 1912. ASV.SS. F.6. 130.

On November 24, Cardinal Merry del Val answered the Minister of Colombia. In regard to the first note the Secretary of State informed the Minister that "such feeling of Colombia concerning the encyclical could not be other than pleasing to the Holy See." He was pleased to inform the Minister that he might acquaint his government of the "very real satisfaction with which His Holiness learned of the favorable, and generous intention" demonstrated by the same government on that occasion. As to the second note, the Cardinal limited himself to thanking the Minister and avoided any judgment about the pamphlet. However, he did add that he thought it timely to state once more the objectives of the aforesaid encyclical.

> This encyclical is truly not directed solely to promoting the religious and civil redemption of the natives existing in a certain immense territory. It is inspired by the universal concern of the Holy Father for all the Indians of Latin America. It responds fully to the salutary pontifical initiative, aimed at regenerating them first of all in the name of Christ, and at defending them, wherever necessary, from the inhuman trading and cruelty to which they are exposed. This general nature or purpose of the encyclical itself shows that it is directed to all the bishops of Latin America. It appears exceedingly appropriate and useful, if one takes into account how much the conditions, more or less painful, according to the various places in which the Indians live, must still, unfortunately, be considered quite widespread. The Holy See, with this initiative, is aiming to hasten the end of so serious a state of affairs. In the new mission of the Putumayo it sees only the beginning of that broad and charitable work which it proposes to carry out gradually in favour of the Indians in Latin America. The Holy See is certain that it is acting in compliance with the humanitarian intention of the governments, and is confident of their cooperation for any undertaking of so great a religious and civil interest.

The Cardinal concluded by saying that the Holy See was "willing to receive with gratitude" the moral and material aid offered by the Colombian government. Moreover, the Holy See would view this as a pledge: "Such an offering would also be the same government's pledge of its favorable dispositions to facilitate later, wherever and however it might be necessary within the boundaries of that very vast republic, the attainment of that object at which the above-mentioned encyclical aims." [15]

---

[15] Cardinal R. Merry del Val to Carmelo Arango, November 24, 1912. ASV.SS. F.6. 2, 3.

Chapter XII

THE MISSIONARIES IN THE PUTUMAYO

The Putumayo Mission Fund appeal slackened during the summer. By October only 2,600 pounds of the 15,000 sought had been raised. Soon, however, Casement received a letter from George Pauling of Victoria Mansions. After expressing his disappointment at how slowly the fund for the Mission was being subscribed to, Pauling highly commended Casement for his "purely humanitarian" motives in this "most excellent work" and announced: "I have great pleasure in offering you such necessary financial support as to enable the Mission to get firmly established and carry on its work." [1]

Genocchi kept in contact with the London committee that was working on the organization of the mission. On October 1, Browne wrote to inform him that the committee expressed the greatest satisfaction with Genocchi's decision to send a lay brother with a knowledge of agriculture and carpentry. They considered the knowledge of tropical agriculture to be of the utmost importance. With this knowledge not only would it be possible to instruct and assist the natives in agriculture and thereby to carry on a valuable civilizing and elevating work, but it would also make the mission largely independent of provisions sent from a long distance. At the same time the members of the committee were working to make arrangements for the missionaries to learn as much about tropical medicine as they possibly could. They were also learning the Spanish language which would be a necessary asset in getting along well with the Peruvians.[2]

On October 10 Browne informed Genocchi that the Prefect of Iquitos, who was in London, told him that "it was very advisable for the proposed mission to get the active support and direct approval of the Peruvian government, otherwise it might be very difficult for the missionaries to get into the Putumayo." He added that "he had no authority or right to give any promise of security, but that [they] should communicate with the government as soon as possible." If they waited

---

[1] George Pauling to R. Casement, December 12, 1912. National Library of Ireland (Dublin), 13073 (quoted by B. L. Reid, *Op. Cit.*, p. 158-159).

[2] P. Browne to G. Genocchi, October 1, 1912. AGG. S.2/B.

until Genocchi and the missionaries arrived in Iquitos, there might be a considerable delay. On the other hand if they were entering the country with "full approval and support of the government," it was certain that no opposition would be shown to the missionaries in their work of establishing the mission in the Putumayo. Browne had written to the English government to request that it help the missionaries in this matter. In accordance with the desire of the committee of the Putumayo Mission Fund, the Foreign Office had sent a telegram to the British representative at Lima. It instructed the representative to inform the Peruvian government of the departure of the mission and to express the "confident hope" of the English government that the Peruvian government would afford it recognition and support because its aim was purely humanitarian. The telegram also stated that the representative should also ask the following: "All reasonable customs facilities for equipment and stores may be afforded to the mission, and should add that [the missionaries] would be most grateful if they could be sent up from Iquitos to the Putumayo in a government launch." Browne asked Genocchi if the Holy See had taken any steps to secure the support and assistance of the Peruvian government.[3]

In his reply, Genocchi stated very briefly that the Holy See had a representative in Lima and that the Peruvian government had a representative in Rome. He did not doubt that the Holy See would take the necessary steps. In any case he would inform the Secretary of State. As to the Prefect of Iquitos, *Señor* Alayza y Paz Soldán, Genocchi said that "for several reasons" one could not put too much trust in him.[4]

Browne wrote to Genocchi that he was glad to hear that the Apostolic Delegate in Lima had been charged to approach the Peruvian government. "I think", he added, "that my government has behaved spendidly in the way it has supported us and in the present endeavours to facilitate the entry and the establishment of the mission."[5] While awaiting the reply of the British minister at Lima, Browne conveyed to Genocchi the views of the committee that the Holy See obtain the assistance of the Peruvian government for the mission. The members of the committee, who knew the country, were "very emphatic in their views as to the absolute necessity" for the mission to have the support of Peru. They affirmed that without this support the mission would meet "innumerable difficulties" in the Putumayo and even in Iquitos. The members were certain that the missionaries would meet covert

---

[3] P. Browne to G. Genocchi, October 10, 1912. ASV.SS. F.5. 42.
[4] G. Genocchi to P. Browne, October 14, 1912. Draft of the letter in ASV.SS. F.5. 44.
[5] P. Browne to G. Genocchi, October 18, 1912. ASV.SS. F.5. 37.

opposition from the Aranas if they did not have the support of the government. Browne therefore asked Genocchi to send him a telegram as soon as he knew that the Apostolic Delegate had obtained the Peruvian government's promise to recognize the mission officially.[6]

Genocchi advised Browne and the members of the committee to use "every precaution" to avoid offending the nationalistic feelings of Peru. He promised that as soon as he received the answer of the Apostolic Delegate he would notify the committee.[7]

On October 29, Browne received a letter from the Foreign Office informing him that the Peruvian government had signified its "willingness to give definite support" to the proposed mission of the Putumayo. They recognized and applauded the purely humanitarian aims of the Church. The mission would be granted "all necessary customs facilities at Iquitos as well as their passage to the Putumayo in a government launch."[8] Thus the ground seemed finally cleared and the departure of the missionaries could be set.

Cardinal Merry del Val cabled Msgr. Scapardini: "Putumayo missionaries accompanied by Genocchi will leave Lisbon for Iquitos November 28."[9] On November 26 Genocchi was in Lisbon. From there he acquainted the Apostolic Delegate at Lima with the details of his mission. The *Huaina* of Booth Company from Liverpool was expected in the evening with the five English missionaries (four priests and one lay brother) who were destined for La Chorrera. The following day Genocchi would embark with them. They would not arrive in Iquitos until after Christmas. If everything went well, Genocchi counted on being in Iquitos around the end of December. He hoped that the authorities would not put any obstacle in the way. Genocchi added that if he felt that his presence in Iquitos was unnecessary to the Franciscans, he planned to leave with the same *Huaina* which would stop in Iquitos for ten or twelve days.[10]

On November 28, Genocchi left Lisbon with the English Franciscan missionaries bound for South America. The Booth Company had given him and his companions free first-class passage together with a gift of 250 pounds and promised all possible cooperation in the future. The missionaries also took with them the personal gift of Pius X, a sum

[6] P. Browne to G. Genocchi, October 22, 1912. ASV.SS. F.5. 40.

[7] G. Genocchi to P. Browne, October 24, 1912. Draft of the letter in ASV.SS. F.5. 41.

[8] P. Browne to the Under Secretary of State, November 1, 1912. PRO. FO. 45070.

[9] Cardinal R. Merry del Val to Msgr. A. Scapardini, November 18, 1912. ASV.DP. F.4. 95.

[10] G. Genocchi to Msgr. A. Scapardini, November 27, 1912. ASV.DP. F.4. 109.

of money and two portable altars. The boat took the travellers directly to their destination and no particular incident occurred en route. They did not know that grave problems awaited them on their arrival, although the Holy See was doing all that it could to prevent disaster.

* * *

On November 21, Msgr. Scapardini cabled Cardinal Merry del Val that the Peruvian government had asked for the approval of the bill which created the diocese of Loreto with the territory of the Prefecture Apostolic of San Léon de Amazonas, and, consequently, with the jurisdiction over the old and new missions. The bill, if it was made by mutual consent, "seemed good" to the Apostolic Delegate. He added that "the government requested an urgent answer, because the Congress [would] terminate its work on December 10." [11] The Secretary of State replied on November 25 with this telegram:

> Telegram of 21 instant received. It is impossible to make a decision on important business, such as creation of diocese, by means of telegraphic communication, and before receiving your report. Moreover it is not a law or Congress which creates dioceses, but Pontifical Act. The Holy See is willing to examine with solicitude the problem of erection of the Diocese of Iquitos, to which your telegram refers. Nevertheless such a diocese could not include the new mission of the Putumayo, already established independently by a decree of the Sacred Congregation for the Propagation of the Faith, because it deals with a non-civilized territory which, further, is disputed by Peru and Colombia. The Holy See cannot be prejudicial to the dispute about the boundaries between the two republics.[12]

Two weeks later the Secretary of State received the report which Msgr. Scapardini had promised in his telegram of November 9. The report explained why the Peruvian government, in accepting the mission in the Putumayo, asked that the diocese of Loreto with its see in Iquitos be erected as soon as possible. The report read: "The President said that we must find a formula which would entitle the government to declare to the Nation that that region [i.e., Putumayo] is Peruvian not only in the political sense but also in the religious sense." [13]

---

[11] Msgr. A. Scapardini to Cardinal R. Merry del Val, November 21, 1912. ASV.DP. F.4. 101.

[12] Cardinal R. Merry del Val to Msgr. A. Scapardini. November 25, 1912. ASV.DP. F.4. 102.

[13] Msgr. A. Scapardini to Cardinal R. Merry del Val, November 10, 1912. ASV.SS. F.6. 27.

The Holy See, conscious of the justice of its cause, took a firm stand against the request of the Peruvian government. On December 13, Cardinal Merry del Val sent to the Apostolic Delegate the following severe instruction:

> Report No. 191/1318 received. According to my repeated instructions, imperative motives of neutrality prevent Holy See from entrusting Putumayo mission either to Peruvian or to Colombian ecclesiastical authorities. The mission was established exclusively for evangelical purpose, without any political ties either to Peruvian or Colombian ecclesiastical authorities. If this government persists in its opposition and Your Excellency with good reason expects further complication, which may disturb religious peace and relationship with Holy See, promptly let me know. In this case I would order missionaries to withdraw or to stop. If this becomes necessary you will make it clear that the responsibility for the failure of the mission, which up until now has received universal praise, necessarily falls on the Peruvian government.[14]

On the following day the Apostolic Delegate sent words of reassurance to the Secretary of State: "At present I do not expect any complication since the government decided to send Minister Goyeneche to Rome to deal personally with the affair of the diocese of Loreto and the Putumayo." [15]

The firmness of the Holy See had obtained its effect. On December 27, the Apostolic Delegate had a meeting with the Peruvian President and the Minister for Foreign Affairs. The President again complained about "the English mission supported by English money" but, at the same time, expressed his desire "not to offend the Holy See." He decided to send Minister Goyeneche to Rome to find a solution for the erection of Loreto as a diocese. He promised that the Peruvian government would grant the missionaries not only the protection of their persons and belongings but also all possible facilities for their civilizing undertaking.[16]

On December 28, a telegram from the Apostolic Delegate brought the news of another difficulty: "Iquitos will receive missionaries hostilely; government promises to oppose but fears serious resistance." [17] In a

---

[14] Cardinal R. Merry del Val to Msgr. A. Scapardini. December 12, 1912. ASV.DP. F.4. 106.

[15] Msgr. A. Scapardini to Cardinal R. Merry del Val, December 13, 1912. ASV.DP. F.4. 107.

[16] Msgr. A. Scapardini to Cardinal R. Merry del Val, December 29, 1912. ASV.DP. F.4. 204.

[17] Msgr. A. Scapardini to Cardinal R. Merry del Val, December 28, 1912. ASV.SS. F.6. 50.

report of George B. Michell, who was the English Consul in Lima, it can be seen that at the beginning of December there had already been a movement afoot at Iquitos to give a hostile reception to the missionaries headed for the Putumayo. On the arrival of the *Atahualpa* on December 5 about 500 members of the populace, headed by *Señor* Nicanor Seavedra (the *Alcalde* of Iquitos in 1911), Carlo Marazzini and other free thinkers arrived at the wharf with the intent of causing a great disturbance. They were very disappointed when Browne, acting as Agent of the Muelle Company, refused to allow them to go down on the pontoon. They were even more disappointed when the priests did not arrive.

On January 11, 1913, Genocchi informed the Apostolic Delegate of his arrival in Iquitos. He added that if they had arrived with the preceding steamship they would have been received poorly by a segment of the population. This segment was especially stirred up by the Italian Carlo Marazzini who played the anticlerical and was the main contributor to the *Antorcha*, an impious and obscene leaflet. After being informed of the unsuccessful demonstration against the English missionaries, the Peruvian government had given very strict orders to the interim Prefect and sent him to Manaus to welcome the missionaries. "For this and for other reasons," Genocchi wrote, "it was an act of grace by Providence that the new prefect boarded with us in Manaus." [18] Genocchi did not specify to the Apostolic Delegate what grace he was granted by Providence at the time of his arrival in Iquitos. Those who blamed Genocchi for the recent developments and regarded him as a rash intruder in their undisturbed tyranny had hired a cut-throat to murder him as soon as he set foot within the forbidden territory. "If my boat had arrived on time," he confided to a friend, "I would have been stabbed to death without ado." A providential storm held up his arrival by one day. The time was enough to enable the government agents to discover the plot and to arrest the would-be assassins.[19]

Genocchi had lengthy conversations with the Prefect Juan José Calle during the nine days from Manaus to Iquitos and during the first week spent in Iquitos. These convinced him that Calle would be the religious and civil salvation of Iquitos. The Prefect had promised to build the church immediately and affirmed that the government would propose to elect the current bishop of Chachapoyas as bishop of Iquitos. In the meantime Calle took pains to obtain the best

---

[18] George B. Michell to E. Grey. January 9, 1913. PRO.FO. 1860.
[19] V. Ceresi, *Op. Cit.*, p. 466.

government steamship that could be found and prepared to conduct the missionaries to La Chorrera. Genocchi strongly emphasized the advantage of choosing English missionaries, reiterating that the Holy See preferred the English not only because of the money raised in England but also for the "honor and good" of Peru. Genocchi felt that soon the missionaries would inform their English friends that there were no irregularities in the Putumayo. After this testimony the English would dismiss "any further plan to send commissions to verify the situation, as public opinion demanded." But had the missionaries been of another nation, "they would not have been easily believed." Moreover, choosing the English would stop the attempt of the Protestant missionaries to come and would avoid the difficulty the Peruvian government would have encountered in dealing with them. Because Genocchi indicated that a Peruvian missionary, named Father Olano, could join the English missionaries, the Prefect commented: "A Peruvian priest would be very desirable in the Putumayo with the English. His presence would much more easily remove any political bias." [20]

Genocchi did not attend the inaugural ceremonies at La Chorrera but preferred to remain at Iquitos. He had already put all the information that he had gathered on his previous visit at the disposal of the new missionaries. His presence at La Chorrera could contribute practically nothing positive to the occasion. Now that the missionaries were in their new field of work at last, in contact with the Indians and their torturers, Genocchi felt that he could withdraw. He had prepared the ground with eighteen months of uninterrupted activity which had been filled with toil, fatigue and dangers. Genocchi would continue to assist this mission, which to a great extent was his own creation, with advice and other useful services. His main task was finished, however, and nothing stood in the way of his prompt return to Europe.

On the way back Genocchi stopped at Rio de Janeiro. There he met with Dr. W. Haggard, the representative of the British government, and gave him the good news. Haggard dispatched this information to his government on February 14, 1913:

> I have seen Father Genocchi on his way to Rome from Iquitos. He was sent by the Pope to inquire into the murders. He is quite persuaded that the new prefect's intention is to stop them by all means possible. They are actually stopped in Putumayo and partially elsewhere except

---

[20] Genocchi to Msgr. A. Scapardini, January 11, 1913. ASV.DP. F.4. 209.

in far distant points not necessarily Peruvian. He is sure that English missionaries will be a great check and that if pressure is not relaxed, the abuses will be stopped altogether.[21]

* * *

On March 7, Genocchi received news from the mission. The missionaries had left Iquitos on January 21 and arrived in La Chorrera on February 3 without any notable incident. They were received by Mr. Juan M. Tizón, general manager of the Arana Company, who placed at their disposal all the necessary facilities for the beginning of the mission. On February 10, the missionaries opened a small school for the native children. They found these Indian children "intelligent and greatly taken with the novelty of being taught." Leaving Father Felix and Father Cyprian to teach in the school, Father Sambrook visited certain sections with Mr. Tizón in order to collect data for a feasible plan of work. On these visits Father Sambrook met many Indians who looked happy and well-fed. Tizón was "very much in earnest" in seeing that all received fair treatment. The missionary also had some discussions with the Police Commissioner who warmly welcomed the missionaries' arrival and was prepared to support any plan of the missionaries for the welfare of the Indians.

Father Sambrook, head of the mission, planned to open another school at El Encanto, the Company's other principal location. At that time there wasn't sufficient work for five missionaries in La Chorrera,

---

[21] W. Haggard to Foreign Office, February 14, 1913. PRO.FO. 7285.

On March 27, 1913, the British Consul at Lima, C. des Graz, transmitted a copy of the first report from the Catholic Mission to the Acting Prefect at Iquitos:

"Apostolic Mission very well received and given every facility for beginning its labours. Impossible in so short time to form an impression as to the nature of the work being carried on by the Casa Arana throughout the Putumayo, but the sections visited by myself appeared to be doing well. The details concerning our work of instruction and civilization will be sent in a letter of the Special Commissary. Father Superior. Leo Sambrook."

The Foreign Office commented: "This is satisfactory. Yes. A resident Roman Catholic Mission is considered to afford the best chance of effecting permanent improvement in the lot of the Indians and it is gratifying to see it has met with a favourable reception." E. Grey sent the following letter to C. des Graz:

"I have received your dispatch No. 44 of March 27th last in which you forward a copy and translation of a telegram received by the Peruvian Ministry of Foreign Affairs from the Acting Prefect at Iquitos transcribing from the Roman Catholic Mission to the effect that they have been well received in the Putumayo district and that their first impression of the present state of affairs is favorable. You should take an opportunity of expressing the appreciation of His Majesty's Government at this communication." PRO.FO. 21805.

Dilecto filio Ioanni Genocchi Congregationis Missionariorum a Sacro Corde Jesu sodali; ob optimam operam in Religionis et humanitatis bonum huic Sanctae Sedi exhibitam praecipue in Americae Meridionalis missione feliciter completa, gratum et benevolentem animum significare volentes, Altaris portatilis privilegium concedimus ita ut, data necessitate, quocumque in loco, congruo tamen et decenti, super idem altare ipse celebrare possit.

Fausta porro et salutaria eidem a Domino adprecantes Apostolicam Benedictionem peramanter impertimus.

Ex aedibus Vaticanis die 19, mense Sextili, anno MCMXIII.

Pius PP. X

and opening a new foundation in El Encanto would give the missionaries access to the white and native population on the Caraparaná. It was not long before the missionaries received the assistance of the older and more intelligent boys, who acted as "monitors" for the younger children. In this way, one of the priests was able to visit the various sections on the days that the Indians came in. In time, he secured their confidence. The priests could switch work from time to time. Apart from the direct good which would result, they could gain useful information to guide them in planning when they would be ready to extend their foundation and to ask for other men from home.[22]

On May 15, further information about the mission reached the Putumayo Mission Fund committee. In a letter addressed to Browne, Father Sambrook stated: "As far as I know at present coercion for rubber is happily a thing of the past." With this good news Father Sambrook told of the missionaries' activities. On March 21, he went to Sur for ten days, visiting a good number of Indian homes, having dinner and spending the night with them. The Indians seemed to take kindly to the *Choveromas,* or "steel men," as they called the English, owing to their *machetes* and tools coming from England. Their attitude was chiefly one of wonder or surprise because the missionaries were the first whites they met who were pledged to celibacy. The Indians appeared quite content and devoted to their chief or *Jefe.* On March 31, Father Sambrook proceeded on a seven hour journey from Sur to Oriente. Here the Okainas tribe lived and worked in the same section. Once again the priest mingled with the Indians and found them much more effusive in their manner than the others Indians he had met. They were also content with their *Jefe.* He returned to La Chorrera on April 9, where the transcription of a Witoto-Spanish dictionary (which the *Jefe* of Sur drew up expressly to help the missionaries) offered sufficient work. On April 24, Fr. Sambrook proceeded to Ultimo Retiro and met all the Indians who had assembled there to bring the rubber which they had gathered in the forest. On the first day of May he visited Occidente where he saw practically all the Indians who were working in that section. Father Felix and Father Cyprian were doing what they could to educate the children in La Chorrera, finding time for occasional visits to Sur and Oriente. Father Frederick suffered five bad attacks of fever. Since the doctor believed that it would only prove fatal for him to remain, he returned to England by the *Liberal.*

---

[22] AGG. L.16/S. L. Sambrook to P. Browne, March 7, 1913. L. Sambrook had sent a copy of his letter to G. Genocchi.

Father Sambrook ended his letter with these remarks:

(1) Each section of the Firm had a very large tract of land under cultivation around the house of the *Jefe*. This supplied himself and the resident Indians with an abundance of fresh food. Each Indian house also had a large tract of land attached to it, likewise under cultivation. In many cases the *chaaras* (as these tracts were called) were enormous and all the Indians looked plump and well-fed.

(2) Each section resembled a small county (there were ten for La Chorrera and nine for El Encanto) and covered an immense stretch of land. The houses of the Indians on the land were quite isolated from each other. The roads were difficult and ravines were spanned by treetrunk bridges. Accordingly, the ultimate aspiration of the mission was to have in each section one missionary whose work would be cut out for him. Meanwhile, the very presence of the missionaries with their frequent visits to the Indians was a strong safeguard of the highest order.

(3) The language spoken by the employers and the Indians who resided around their houses was Spanish. These Indians were called *muchachos* and served as foremen. Hardly 5 per cent of the other Indians spoke Spanish. Each Indian spoke his own language. Of these languages, the one most extensively used was Huitoto, which the Recigoras, Boras, and Okainas also spoke in addition to their own. The missionaries were beginning with Huitoto which was very complicated.

(4) As soon as possible they began to do at El Encanto along the Caraparaná what they were doing on the Igaraparaná.

In his letter Father Sambrook mentioned the report by George B. Michell, who was British Consul in Iquitos, of a tour carried out by him in the Putumayo district. This had been issued as a parliamentary paper on April 4, 1913, and was published in the English newspapers on April 5. The missionary informed his London correspondent: "Feelings are high in Iquitos owing to the statement made in the English newspapers." They were "eagerly translated" and given a prominent place in the Putumayo papers. Nevertheless, Father Sambrook noticed that rumors were linked with those statements of a fortune at the missionaries' backs and a great deal of other false testimony against the missionaries.[23]

---

[23] L. Sambrook to P. Browne, May 15, 1913. PRO.FO. 33320.

G. Michell who made the tour in company with Fuller, the United States Consul in Iquitos, had arrived at the following conclusions with regard to the working conditions in the Putumayo. No evidence of cruelties being perpetrated at that time came to his notice, the policy of the Company having been changed for the better under *Señor* Tizón's management. Their fairly satisfactory state depended largely upon continuing the policy of the Company's present agents at La Chorrera and El Encanto. It also depended on the development, faithful application and maintenance of the new proposals of the Peruvian government. G. Michell mentioned that, among various reforms, Tizón had abolished the payment of commissions on the quantity of rubber furnished by the Indians. Instead, they received a fixed salary. The British Consul was permitted to see the Company's account books. All these measures apparently had a very satisfactory effect. The Consul stated: "It is confidently asserted by all the Company's agents that no cruelties or compulsion are now being exercised on the natives throughout the Putumayo: we certainly saw no evidence of barbarities during our journey." With regard to the establishment of a mission, *Señor* Arana, *Señor* Loayza and Tizón expressed themselves entirely in favor of the proposal. They also said that they would facilitate in every possible way the founding and carrying on of schools for the Indian children.[24]

* * *

On September 20, 1913, Father Sambrook sent to Genocchi the first draft of the report which he was preparing for the Prefect of the Congregation for the Propagation of the Faith. After thanking Genocchi for his letter and for the "cheering news" regarding the Holy Father's improvement in health, Father Sambrook apologized for the delay in writing. The *Liberal* came only three or four times a year and remained a very short time on each trip. Consequently, letters had to wait in Iquitos until the departure of the next ocean-going vessel. Thus, not only was it absolutely impossible to send letters often, but they had to be answered quickly. Frequently these answers remained in Iquitos an indefinite length of time before being dispatched to their destination.

Father Sambrook informed Genocchi that so far they had received "nothing but kindness" from the employees of the Firm. They were all doing everything they could to further the missionaries' work. He gave a brief summary of the facts that would be enlarged upon in the report that he was preparing for the Congregation.

---

[24] *The Times*, April 5, 1913.

(1) The Indians — men, women, children — numbered between 8,000 and 10,000. The proportion of adults over children was noticeable. The white element was roughly 100.

(2) The Indians spoke some six or seven completely different languages, the most common of which was Huitoto.

(3) The Indians of each part were divided into twenty sections for the purpose of work. Out of these sections, eleven were on the Igaraparaná and nine on the Caraparaná. The sections on the Igaraparaná were larger and contained more natives. Generally the natives lived in their huts at great distances from each other and from the house of the white employer. This lack of concentration made it practically impossible to do much for them. On the Caraparaná, certain sections were concentrated into small towns like colonies; the houses of the Indians were situated around the houses of the manager of the section. Unfortunately in these cases the colonies were very small: some one hundred Indians in all, including men, women and children.

(4) The adults held on to their old ideas and, from what Father Sambrook had seen and heard, they did not want to change them in favor of a new religion. Moreover, as they had religious ideas which imposed no moral obligations, they were unwilling to accept the positive obligations of the Christian religion. Parents were devoted to their children and did not like the idea of handing them over to a missionary to be educated. They were willing to part with orphans. The main vices of the Indians were sexual passion, indolence, inconstancy and theft. In these circumstances, the only feasible plan which the missionaries could follow at the time was to choose some new centers for grouping the children of the Indians and the orphans of the region. There were difficulties in connection with this plan, but the missionaries were earnestly studying how to overcome them. Meanwhile, the main problem was that in this territory (which was as large as England and split up into twenty areas of work, each the size of a province) dwelt a population only one-half that of Iquitos. As already noted, the Indians (whose adult population far exceeded the children's) lived their isolated lives in houses quite far from each other and spoke six or seven different languages.[25]

On January 14, 1914, Father Sambrook sent a detailed report of the mission to Cardinal Prefect Girolamo Gotti, Prefect of the Congregation for the Propagation of the Faith. The report was one of

---

[25] L. Sambrook to G. Genocchi, September 20, 1913. AGG. L.16/S.

those which the Congregation was accustomed to receive from the missions scattered throughout the world. It dealt with the location of the mission (geographical and ethnographical data), with the difficulties and with the program of the mission. Only one segment of the report is of particular importance here. When Father Sambrook dealt with the treatment of the mission and natives, he stated:

> The treatment given to our mission is quite excellent up to the present, since our Fathers receive all the facilities and every consideration both from the Company itself in Iquitos and from their workers in this region. The treatment of the natives seems humane to me. The relations with them are such as can expected between civilized men and native savages, and they seem to be quite content.[26]

This remark of Father Sambrook, which appears almost peripheral to the context of his report, shows clearly the change which had taken place with the establishment of the missionaries in that region which was called "The Devil's Paradise." After only one year of the missionaries' presence, the atrocities and slavery were completely eradicated. The evangelization of the Indians followed the routine of the evangelization of all primitive peoples, with its problems and its hopes. In Father Sambrook's correspondence with his English Superior and with the Prefect of the Congregation there was no complaint about abuse by the rubber traders in the years that followed.

Father Genocchi would very soon give back his commission as willingly as he had received it. His reward was one which a servant of the Church, as he considered himself, can appreciate — the sincere expression of complete satisfaction by its head on earth, the Vicar of Christ. Apart from all else, proof that he did receive such a reward is to be found in the letter which Pius X wrote to him in his own hand after Genocchi's return from the Putumayo. He granted him the privilege (at that time very rare) of a portable altar for the rest of his life. The Pontifical document read:

> To our beloved son, Giovanni Genocchi, a member of the Congregation of the Missionaries of the Sacred Heart of Jesus, as a sign of our grateful appreciation for his excellent achievement on behalf of religion and humanity, and in particular for the assignment successfully carried out in South America under the auspices of the Holy See, we grant the privilege of the portable altar in any fitting and suitable place. With deep

---

[26] AGG. L.16/S. L. Sambrook to Cardinal G. Gotti, January 14, 1914. L. Sambrook had sent a copy of his letter to G. Genocchi.

affection we grant him our Apostolic blessing and pray that the Lord continue to bless and sustain him.[27]

Genocchi was happy with the fatherly appreciation expressed to him by the Pope who had sent him, but much more in having served the Vicar of Christ in one of his more generous undertakings. Most of all, he was happy to have cooperated with the Pope in the writing of one of the most beautiful pages in the history of civilization and Christian charity, thus vindicating the honor of the human family which had been so compromised by the atrocities of the Putumayo.

---

[27] "Dilecto filio Joanni Genocchi Congregationis Missionariorum a Sacro Corde Jesu sodali, ob optimam operam in Religionis et humanitatis bonum huic Sanctae Sedis exhibitam praecipue in Americae Meridionalis missione feliciter completa, gratum et benevolentem animum significare volentes, Altaris portatilis privilegium concedimus ita ut, data necessitate, quocumque in loco, congruo tamen et decenti, super idem altare ipse celebrare possit.

Fausta porro et salutaria eidem a Domino adprecantes Apostolicam Benedictionem peramanter impertimus.

Ex Aedibus Vaticanis die 19, mense Sextili, anno MIMXIII.

Pius PP. X

AGG. L.15/P.

APPENDIX

CHRISTIANITY AND SLAVERY*

The relationship between Christianity and slavery imbues eighteen centuries of history, not only with facts but also and particularly with ideas and with social psychology. Without going into a treatise now, I will summarily put together bits of information, outlining a picture, to which my alert listeners will be able easily to add color and life.

First, let us glance at slavery in the civilized world at the advent of Christianity. The condition of the slaves among the pagans is all too clear now — horrible for many, most wretched for all. What was thought, at that time, of the lawfulness of slavery? Premises varied, but they always led to conclusions hallowed by lengthy arguments of Aristotle, the logician par excellence, the master of learning: "Civilization without slavery is not possible. God wills the distinction between master and slave, as he wills the distinction between male and female. *Therefore nature determines female and slave.*" [1] It is true that some, especially the Stoics, denied that nature itself made the distinction. They held, however, that the intrinsic make-up of civil society required it, and this came down to a question of words which did not change the given principle: *slavery is absolutely indispensable to a civilized society.*

Now we must ask ourselves: Assuming, as we must, this very firm and universal conviction, was there ever a pagan who considered slavery unjust even though he recognized it as a social necessity? Indeed. There was Epictetus, the philosopher and slave, whose leg was broken by his master Epafroditus. One day Epafroditus, one of Nero's chosen guards, began, just as a whim, to twist his slave's leg. The slave calmly said to him, "Be careful, for if you keep it up, you will break it." The brute went right on and actually broke it. And the slave remarked, "Didn't I tell you it would end like this?" — an admirable disposition of a philosopher slave, an exception as remarkable as it is rare. It is not, then, at all surprising that so noble a soul with such an experience should consider slavery a great injustice and indicate so in his writings.

---

* Lecture read by Father G. Genocchi at the second Italian Anti-slavery convention, held in Rome on December 3-4, 1907.

[1] *Politics* I, 1,5. ὡσει μὲν οὖν διώρισται τὸ θῆλυ καὶ δοῦλον. Cf. *Ibid.* VIII, 2.

Seneca protested slavery in the name of humanity, but these were
protests in vain, as when in our time we call it an injustice that the
worker should sweat in the shop while the rich man sits idly on a
feather pillow. But, effectively, what could be done about it? The voices
of Seneca and Epictetus, isolated and to a great extent very timid
voices, were voices crying in the wilderness. They left not even a
fleeting echo behind them.

In addition, we find in the history of paganism no movement
which could have led to the abolition of slavery, nor the living seed
which could have developed into an anti-slavery movement. Against
certain atrocious cruelties of masters, laws were promulgated by
Augustus, perhaps by Nero if the Petronian Law is from this period, by
Domitian, Hadrian and Antonius Pius; but no one passed a law that
would lead to the abolition of slavery. They pruned the poisonous tree,
but did not decide to axe its roots.

Still the question remains: if Christianity had not arisen, would
slavery have ever been abolished? Only at the end of this talk can we
attempt to answer this difficult question.

Now let us see if and how Christianity is anti-slavery. The Founder
of our religion based the moral in charity: Love God above all things
and your neighbor as yourself. This principle is also found in other
religions and other philosophies but it is lost and suffocated by all sorts
of rules. Jesus Christ made charity the only law of His religion, while all
other dogmatic and moral norms exist only to strengthen and maintain
it. God is the Father, we are all brothers. There is no true father or lord
except the Heavenly Father. As if that were not enough, Jesus Christ
has found a way to make sacred the exercise of charity towards one's
brothers, since he who does good to the least of men for love of Him,
does good to Him; and he who offends his brothers, offends Him. And
then there is Paul who preaches *"non est Judaeus neque Graecus, non est
servus neque liber, non est masculus neque foemina. Omnes enim vos unum estis in
Christo Jesu"* [2] [There is neither Jew nor Greek, there is neither slave
nor freeman, there is neither male nor female, for you are all one in
Christ Jesus.] There were also the example of the Master, who, being
God, "had taken the form of a slave" and had chosen and ennobled the
attitudes and tortures and death of a slave.[3] To slaves alone was
reserved, for example, the service of washing feet, the pain of scourging
and the agony of the cross. Certain dispositions befitting slaves, such as
resignation and humility, never listed by philosophers among the

---

[2] Gal. 3:28.
[3] Phil. 2:7.

virtues, were raised by Christ to the honor of qualities required of His disciples.

So, Christians filled with this spirit, finding themselves in a society composed of masters and slaves, began to put the Gospel precepts into practice. As is natural, they neither changed the milieu nor upset the existing social structure. The master-slave structure remained. But the Christian master could no longer consider his slave inferior by nature, without rights, to be trampled upon with impunity; he was rather a brother destined by Providence to menial tasks, not ignoble however, for they had been sanctified by Jesus Christ. Mistreating a slave was the same sin as mistreating Jesus Christ, although it was not at all a sin to keep him in the condition established for him by the Heavenly Father. The slave, too, was the son of the Heavenly Father with the same title as the master. To show kindness and courtesy to a slave was to show it to Jesus Christ, who was then to judge man principally on charity, or even solely on charity, according to Mt. 25. A slave who became a Christian (and the master was to do his utmost to bring this about) gave his master the kiss of peace at the same Eucharistic meal and was on a par with him, with absolutely no distinction, in Church assemblies. In addition, nothing prevented a virtuous and capable slave from becoming a priest, a bishop or even a Pope. St. Callistus I was a fugitive slave; St. Pius I, a brother of the slave Erma, must, therefore, have himself been a slave. Evaristus and Anicetus were names of slaves, and they very likely were freedmen. Moreover, Blandina of Lyons, Felicita of Carthage, and Potamiena of Egypt, all slaves, were some of the most celebrated heroines among the martyrs of the first centuries. How many slaves, both men and women, earned the crown of martyrdom! When the Christian society began to breathe in the peace of Constantine, the learned Lactantius, after making a kind of examination of conscience of Christianity, could write: "*Apud nos nemo clarissimus, nisi qui opera misericordiae largiter fecerit ...; inter servos et dominos interest nihil; nobis invicem fratrum nomen impertimus, quia pares esse nos credimus*" [4] [Among us no one is noteworthy except those who magnanimously perform works of mercy; there is no difference whatsoever between slaves and masters; we call each other brother, because we believe we are all equal.]

Nonetheless slavery remained and Christianity did not abolish it. Christians of the first centuries did not even consider doing so. It did not cross their minds. But would it possibly have crossed the minds of the great apostles, saints and doctors of that time? I will not give the answer, which would perhaps seem rash, but I will take it verbatim

---

[4] Lact. *Div. Iust.* V, 14.

from Balmes, that great Catholic genius of modern Spain, whose work on Christianity and Slavery is a model of learning, piety and beauty: "It is by no means necessary that the merit of this conduct toward slaves was understood by those who took part in it. It is not even necessary to suppose that the first Christians understood all the force of the tendencies of Christianity with respect to the abolition of slavery. What is required to be shown is, that the result has been obtained by the doctrines and conduct of the Church." [5]

Therefore, let us also in all fairness admit, according to the evidence of the documents, that in early centuries, indeed for many centuries, Christians considered slavery necessary to society and, therefore, did not consider abolishing it. But all believed it to be a very strict obligation of Christians to treat slaves as equal to themselves by nature, indeed as brothers, sons of the same Father God and as the faithful redeemed by Jesus Christ, the severe judge of offenses done to slaves as offenses against Himself. Well, then, was this still slavery in the pagan sense, i.e. where the slave had no human rights, had only a half human soul (as Homer and Plato claim), was nothing but an instrument with life (as Aristotle declares), was at the mercy of his master, who ruled his slaves as absolutely as he ruled his dogs or donkeys? No, slavery continued because Christians did not yet know how to replace it; but it had become more an embarrassment than a satisfaction for the masters. Having slaves and having to treat them with so much regard was, frankly, more of a loss than a gain. These gentlemen slaves, brothers in Christ to their masters, with the rights of other Christians, in fact with more rights than others (the Gospel gives more rights and divine compassion to the little ones than to the great, to the lowly than to the mighty), no longer served to satisfy without limit the sensuality, the arrogance, the greed of masters. If humankind, unreformed by Christian principles, prefers having slaves, it does so precisely to satisfy the three ingrained instincts of pleasure, sensuality and greed. But to fulfillment of these instincts requires a slave in the true sense of the word, the *slave-thing* as in paganism, not the *slave-man* or *slave-brother* as found only in Christianity. In fact, if we observe well, the slave still being called *servus*, *doulos* among Christians, was no longer the slave in the old sense, but was another being altogether and brought to mind a concept quite different from the old one. Christians, in order to evoke the pagan idea of slave, could no longer say *servus*, *doulos*, but had to find new terms. The old word survived to meam *servants* but has

---

[5] J. Balmes, *European Civilization* (New York: J. Murphy Co., 1850), p. 94.

nothing to do with the classical *servus*; while *slave* came into use for historical reasons which we do not have time to elaborate upon.

So Christianity soon changed the concept of slave and rendered the Christian slave as a contradiction in terms. The contradictions between things and principles, when the principles have the force of religion and are rooted in sentiment, end up falling into ruin; and the things die while the principles triumph, despite the work of those who refuse to accept them. As soon as social and economic conditions would permit, slavery, undermined by Christianity, would fall apart and disappear, as in fact it did little by little, without laws, without violences, by slow and spontaneous disintegration.

As to the question put at the beginning of this talk, whether slavery would ever have been abolished without Christianity, we must reply that this kind of prediction cannot be made in history. But we cannot ascertain what ideas and what events, except the Gospel, could have made slavery first almost useless and then absolutely repugnant to civil society, which had derived so many advantages from it. Let us put aside speculations, in themselves misleading, and stick scientifically to facts.

Only Christianity has given mankind an understanding of universal fraternity and has made man lose the idea of the *slave-thing*, making slavery almost useless and fundamentally abhorrent. This development was immensely more significant than would have been a precept by Jesus Christ abolishing slavery; for that would have either produced a catastrophe or rendered His Religion unacceptable. Jesus, with divine wisdom, planted a seed, all the hidden forces of which not even the most competent farmers could imagine. The seed sprang up and in time produced, among other fruits the abolition of slavery. Another indispensable fact is that the strongest and most effective campaign against the slave trade and slavery in general was waged because of the Christian principle. One example, among many, suffices to illustrate this fact — an example which is the most commendable one I know on the subject. It is now a century since the English House of Commons (February 23, 1807) approved the abolition of the slave trade, thanks to the work of that great Christian Wilberforce. He exclaimed on that day of his triumph, that he had never felt so much gratitude as when he realized the great goal of his life towards which Providence had been guiding him for twenty-seven years. The decree received the royal signature on March 25 of the same year, on the feast of the Incarnation of the Redeemer, which had brought brotherhood to the world. In 1833, the same English House of Commons voted abolition not only of slave trade but of slavery itself, setting aside 20,000,000 pounds sterling for the cause and writing one of the most glorious pages of English history. This was due to Buxton, supported by the Christian movement, especially the efforts of English women dedicated to the name of Christ and His Gospel.

Therefore, when one fights for slavery, one does so in the name of pagan selfishness, as presently the school of Nietzsche does. When one fights for the abolition of slavery and for universal freedom, either it is openly in the name of Christ and the Gospel (as this worthy anti-slavery society), or it is at least under the influence (at times manifest, at times hidden, but always true and authentic) of those principles of liberty, fraternity and equality which the Gospel brought to, and nourishes in, the world.

TIPOGRAFIA POLIGLOTTA DELLA PONTIFICIA UNIVERSITÀ GREGORIANA
PIAZZA DELLA PILOTTA, 4 - ROMA